don't fret

THE
WORSHIP LEADER'S POCKETBOOK

DON PURDEY

Don't Fret: The Worship Leader's Pocketbook

Author: Don Purdey

© 2020

dontfretbook.com

Cover Design: Ruth Grace

Published by: Annette Purdey

September 2020

ISBN: 978-0-6488567-0-2 (sc)

ISBN: 978-0-6488567- 1-9 (ePub)

ISBN: 978-6488567-2-6 (kindle)

A catalogue record for this work is available from the National Library of Australia

To God be the glory

CONTENTS

FOREWORD

I remember standing at the back of a gathering of ministers and leaders. When church leaders and pastors get together they know how to sing – boisterously! Next to me was my colleague and friend and the author of this book. By now, the symptoms of Motor Neurone Disease were evident in his slurred speech, and equally noticeable when he sang. Yet, despite his duress, the physical effort required to voice each word, I will never forget the energy, passion and spirit with which he sang. There was no more fervent worshipper in the room.

Don't Fret emerges from Don's love of worship so amply demonstrated that day. His passion for worship is born of his devotion to his Lord. 'I love to worship God', he says, 'and I really love being in the midst of a room full of Jesus' disciples who are giving their all in their love for Jesus.'

There are good reasons to read this book. It has come out at a time when churches diet on a continual stream of popular and stylistically relevant worship songs from predominantly globally recognised labels. In some ways we are spoilt for choice and quality. Some of these songs will be as timeless and classic as those few that emerged from the many written and sung in the eras of the Wesleys, Billy Graham or charismatic renewal songsters such as Keith Green or Amy Grant.

Amidst our contemporary richness of music and song, Don threads through his book a reminder that the focus of our worship ought to be on God, not as our 'benevolent helper', but God for who he is: 'Too many people come to worship seeking an experience for themselves rather than seeking to glorify God.'

Not that this is a theological treatise on worship. Far from it. Don looks for theological 'reliability', but the primary role of this book is to provide an accessible, practical guide for those preparing and presenting services of worship. For those new to the craft, here is a valuable overview of the elements that make up a worship event and what they mean.

For those designers of worship - newbies or old hands - who want to break the week to week routine and are intentionally seeking to discover the flow, direction and power that provides God's people with the opportunity to truly worship, this is such a helpful resource. From worship leader responsibilities, to copyright obligations and record-keeping to testing cables, connections and batteries to the choice of lyrics and the positioning of songs and prayers, to subtle key shifts, Don has it covered. I've rarely seen these things brought together so comprehensively, yet so accessibly.

Don provides brief analysis of the significant elements of worship. Yet he is careful not to reduce his examination of these to a kind of formulaic process. The context is always ministry in the Spirit and the author is not backward in describing experiences of the supernatural presence of God.

On the day Don died, 23 July 2014, his computer was open to the last page of this book where he quotes 2 Timothy 4:6-8. According to Annette, he had obviously been applying finishing touches on the day he died.

I'm glad Don wrote this book. Perhaps he needed to. It's a simple, readable guide to worship. It's a legacy from a pastor, worship leader, musician, who wanted to leave something for those who have, like him, a heart for ministry and worship.

Underneath it all is a narrative of a life lived in service to Christ and who is now, in his own words, 'at peace with God'.

Craig Bailey

Director of Leadership

Uniting College for Leadership & Theology, Adelaide

PREFACE

Although I knew that Dad was writing a practical book on Worship, I actually never laid eyes on a page until after Dad passed away suddenly in 2014. Aside from the grief of the loss, it was a shame I never got to discuss it with him; it was obvious he just wanted to be happy with the draft himself before he showed it to family.

If you flip to the very last section of the book you'll see the first part I read of this Worship Leader's Pocketbook—and a Bible verse that will never be the same for me:

> *"For I am already being poured out like a drink offering...I have fought the good fight, I have finished the race, I have kept the faith. Now there is in store for me the crown of righteousness..."*
> *(2 Timothy 4:6-8)*

Dad was diagnosed with Motor Neurone Disease (MND) in early 2011, and it was this that necessitated his retirement as a Church minister and worship leader. This was obviously a huge blow not only to him but our whole family. However, his faith in Jesus shone out even in this difficult time, because he was assured God works all things for the good of those who love him. This pocketbook, therefore, had come about because Dad suddenly had lots of time to reflect on a lifetime of leading God's people in worship. He was able to put together some practical tips to help people learn from the wisdom given him, as well as mistakes made along the way.

In fact, what he really wanted was a book that was quick and easy to read. His final draft even included pre-highlighted parts as he wanted to make it as easy to read as possible. Although we had to change a few things inevitably in the drafting process (incredibly hard when the author is not able to reply to comments), we have left it as untouched as possible so the message he wanted to express would come across loud and clear. In fact, this was our real difficulty in finishing the book—so you'll excuse us for taking a couple of years longer than we would have liked.

I write this preface on behalf of all our family, and we all pray this for you: May this book bless you as much as the man who wrote it blessed our family, friends, church, and many across Australia. And, as Dad would have wanted it: To God be the glory.

Malcolm Purdey

September 2020

INTRODUCTION

Church worship has undergone a dramatic shift in the course of my lifetime. The world of hymns, choirs, formal prayers from books and eloquent or obscure sermons delivered from high pulpits by robed clergy that I grew up with, has largely given way to amplified bands, casual dress, lay-led worship and conversational messages.

In the midst of those changes, the way that church services are planned has undergone serious modification. Previously, services were constructed by the professionals—the priests and ministers and pastors who had received theological instruction and were placed by their denominations into mostly established churches to lead worship and pastor the flock. They crafted their services using hymn books, prayer books, flowery responsive liturgies and the strictness of denominational doctrine.

These days many new churches have sprung up, many not affiliated with any denomination, and more and more we see that even the denominational professional (if there is one) is delegating the construction of the service to others, which is not necessarily bad. Worship is relaxed and even casual, the traditions stripped away to leave little beyond singing, sermons and prayer.

Another consequence of these changes is that many of the people who are shaping their church's worship don't always completely grasp what they are doing. Either they unthinkingly copy a model of worship that they inherited, or they gleefully tear an old model apart, but all too frequently both can happen without the instigators really knowing what they are doing or why. New congregations may even copy current trends in worship without ever considering the role that each part might play in the worship they construct.

The way worship is delivered has also undergone a similar shift, from the old two-man show of priest and organist to the current multi-faceted productions. The "hymn sandwich" has been replaced by multi-media presentations with often quite long periods of singing and far less attention to prayer and other facets of worship.

So, this book is designed to help those who are now preparing and presenting their church's service to "ground" what they are doing. We'll look at what constitutes a worship service and how to build a service that flows both logically and spiritually. We'll also address the presentation of worship and especially music, all in a way that I hope is practical and helpful.

This is not intended as a theology book, nor as a theology of worship, though I hope it gives a helpful glimpse into those areas. Many people far better qualified than I have written books on theology and worship! Instead, my hope is that this little book will end up in the hip pockets and handbags—or on the tablets and e-readers—of people who are engaged in helping the people of God worship him week by week. Whether you are a ministry professional or a dedicated lay person, my intention is for this book to be a brief, practical and helpful guide that you can refer to quickly, spending your precious time doing your part in ministry and not just reading about it.

The book grew out of a number of seminars and teaching sessions on worship, worship music and worship leading skills that I gave in various contexts as part of my ministry. Now that illness has forced me to retire from the pressures of parish life I have had a chance to reflect on the material in my old notes and develop it into a more useful form. It comes with over thirty years of experience in presenting music for worship gained from many successes, a few triumphs, and, yes, many mistakes. Also, in here are some things from my sixteen years of ordained ministry, including the "in hindsight" department: looking back, I wish I had done some things differently at times. I hope you can learn from it all.

Worship is a personal—even intimate—subject for us. So what constitutes good worship varies with every individual. I put forward my particular view in this book. You may disagree with me, and that's fine. In deciding what you think, you will at least have wrestled with the issues I raise and in doing so sharpened your own opinions on the whetstone of mine.

As I said, it's designed as a pocket manual. That doesn't only refer to the size. I have tried to set the book out with sensible section and chapter headings, keeping it all as concise as I can. I have also tried to highlight some of the key phrases in bold so that your eye will spot them quickly and you will find the bit you're hunting for. It really is designed with active ministry in mind, so that you can share the appropriate bits with your team and get yourselves onto the same page. Of course, I hope you'll convince them to read all the pages!

I pray as you go about preparing and delivering your ministry—leading worship among the people—that what I have written will bless and guide you. If it does, give the glory to God; if it doesn't, I pray that at least it will have offered you enough to start you thinking on some key issues. I want to encourage you to keep striving for your answers not just here but also in other places until you feel competent and confident to fulfil your role.

I dedicate this work to you, and to everyone on your worship team, as you seek to bring glory to God.

1 THE WHAT AND WHY OF WORSHIP

WHAT IS WORSHIP?

Many books have explored the question of what constitutes worship. It's not one that we can rattle off a single sentence answer to with any satisfaction. My purpose here is to offer a brief survey of what worship has come to mean for the Christian church so that we have a basis upon which the rest of this pocketbook can unfold.

We could turn to the dull definitions of the noun *worship* in the dictionary, describing it as "worthiness, merit, recognition given or due to these, honour and respect," and as a verb, "adore as divine, pay religious homage to, idolize, regard with adoration," and finally, "reverence paid to God… in church service."[1]

How can dictionaries make something so amazing sound so lifeless? While these definitions can start us on the path to understand worship, they are so dry, especially when as Christians we want to fully embrace it. Worship for me is a concept that engages the whole body, mind and spirit. I really like William Temple's description when he writes:

---

[1] *The Concise Oxford Dictionary of Current English* (7th Edition), (1982) Ed. J. B. Sykes, Oxford University Press, Oxford.

To worship is:
To quicken the conscience by the holiness of God
To feed the mind with the truth of God
To purge the imagination by the beauty of God
To open the heart to the love of God
To devote the will to the purpose of God.[2]

Yet even that profound insight to me has it slightly backward, as its emphasis seems to me to fall more on what we receive from God when we worship—which is understandable! As a minister I would often have people say to me at the door on the way out, "I got a lot out of worship today." I was glad they had benefited, but the point of worship is not to gain for ourselves, but to honour God. Too many people come to worship seeking an experience for themselves rather than seeking to glorify God.

I look at it this way. **Worship is first a choice we make, and then an action we take**. Worship first and foremost is we, the people, choosing to honour God because of who he is. We choose to recognise God—Father, Son and Spirit—and then we act on that choice by bending our knees to him in humility and reverence, and living through him and for him. **It occupies our whole life**. It is afterward, when we look back on living out our life of worship, that we realise the blessings we have received in return. So for me, our heart's desire in **worship is to offer all that we are in honour of all who God is.**

Years ago, I wrote a song trying to express this notion. It's not a "known" song as to my knowledge it hasn't been used outside my own congregations, but I print it here simply so that you'll grasp my point more clearly:

---

[2] William Temple, *The Hope of a New World* (1941), as cited by Dr Nick Hawkes, *The Bible on the Key Issues of Life*, 2013, Even Before Publishing, Capalaba, Qld.

You're all that is good
You're all that is perfect
You're all that is holy
You're all that is wise
You're all that is mighty
You're all that is lovely
You're all that's majestic
You're all that's sublime

Father I worship You
With all of my mind
Jesus I come to You
With all of my heart
Spirit, come flow through me
Lay open my soul
So all that's within me
Can praise all that You are.[3]

As Paul put it so wonderfully in Romans 12, to offer our bodies as living sacrifices is a spiritual act of worship. To me, that means that I can consider all that I am, and all that I do, as worship. **Every facet of my life can be counted as an opportunity to worship the God who created me, saved me and loves me**.

Worship of God is the most important thing we do. **Our Christian faith defines us**. Often when we are getting to know people we will ask, "What do you do?" And the answer will be a doctor or a teacher or a shop attendant or whatever. And if we are a Christian, we become known as a Christian doctor, or a Christian teacher.

That has it all backwards. We are not defined by what we do—especially in God's eyes. You aren't a teacher who happens to be a Christian. You are a Christian who happens

---

[3] "All That You Are", © 1990 Don Purdey.

13

to be a teacher, or a doctor or whatever. You are a doctor Christian, or a teacher Christian. And your whole life is given for the purpose of glorifying God.

So whether I am an artist, or a shop assistant, or a plumber, or a computer programmer, or a farmer, or a house-husband, or a nurse, or a factory hand, my daily work would be worship, my interactions with my fellow workers would be worship, my love for my family would be worship, the way I spoke my words and disciplined my home life would be worship, the whole way that I conducted my life would be a part of my means of honouring God. Because it is my faith that defines me and **worship is my true purpose**.

So worship can and should encompass every activity of our lives. Yet, as we saw from the dictionary, we also use the word to indicate what happens in a church service. It is that other definition that is the focus of this book.

What we do in a church service is, in a sense, an attempt to mimic in a corporate way the worship that we offer as individuals. The intent is the same: to glorify God. And the process is the same too: we take all that we have available among us and offer it together to God in honour of him. We want to apply our minds, our creativity, our skills, our hearts, our emotions, our passion, our bodies and our wills to this joint opportunity to fulfil the first commandment, that we love God with heart, soul, mind and strength.

Church worship is a freewill offering from a congregation of the people of God to the Lord they love and serve. And in saying that, I am also saying that it is NOT what it sometimes appears to be: a carefully programmed performance put on by a preacher, a choir or band and a few chosen leaders. **If the congregation in their hearts and minds are separating themselves from what is being done at the front on their behalf then the service has failed in its most important duty.**

Worship in church is an amazing blessing, as it brings the heartfelt desire of many to honour their God together in a blessed unity. It fulfils a longing within us to unite with like-minded people and join with them to amplify all that is within us. We derive pleasure and satisfaction from blending with others for this supreme purpose.

Worship leader and vocalist Darlene Zschech describes walking into a church service shortly after her conversion with her "new heart and spirit" (Ezekiel 36:26) this way:

> *...here it was, the sound of one voice, one heart, one song, a sound that was more spiritual than musical, and a sound that was very beautiful... it was the sound of the church at worship... it's the sound that everyone was born to recognise and contribute to...* [4]

Most of us can probably recall a worship occasion that has been the pinnacle of our experience. For me, it came at a conference featuring John Wimber in Sydney in 1991. Five thousand Christians had gathered and they sang with all their hearts, not the latest modern song but an older tune, "Holy, holy, holy, Lord, God of power and might, heaven and earth are full of your glory, hosanna, hosanna in the highest". Some describe a mist, some say smoke, but whatever you call it, there was a whitish haze across the room that for me was the tangible presence of God in the old Hordern Pavilion of the Sydney Showground. There was a great band, and a really gifted worship leader, but it's not just those people who made that moment special for me. It was ultimately those five thousand voices, joining as one in honour of their Lord. **When worship is at its best, it is a freely given, thankful and joyful outpouring of the whole gathered body of Christ, focussed solely on their Lord.**

---

[4] Darlene Zschech: "The True Value of Worship", YouTube video.

Worship is made up of a number of elements. Some people think of words like praise, thanksgiving, piety and worship as interchangeable descriptions of the same thing. I don't think that's the case. The words each have distinct meanings and nuances that are important to consider when we are preparing and conducting worship.

Thanksgiving is a part of worship. Obviously, from its name, it's about the way in which we give thanks to God for what he has done. Psalm 100 says to enter his gates with thanksgiving (Psalm 100:4); it is a wonderful way to commence worship. We should include thanksgiving in worship, but worship is more than just thanksgiving.

Piety is a part of worship. Piety is when we express our devotion to God and our desire to live in his ways and for his purposes, perhaps like David often did (for example, Psalm 26). It is a description of our response to God and it is good to do that in worship, but worship is more than just telling God of our intention to follow him.

Praise is a part of worship. Praise is when we talk about God and list off some of the many things we love about him, like many of the Psalms do (for example, Psalm 96). Praise in our churches is about celebrating God's wonderful attributes. Praise is a key part of worship, but worship is more than praise alone.

Worship, in its purest sense, is when we submit ourselves fully and directly to God and adore him. It is when we join with the angels and all the company of heaven and cry, "Holy, holy, holy is the Lord God Almighty, who was and is and is to come." (Revelation 4:8)

Worship alone is for God. We can give thanks to lots of people for lots of gifts or circumstances, we can praise many people and situations, and we can piously follow a political party, a football team or someone important to us—like a dedicated parent. They are terms not specifically set apart for God quite in the way that the word "worship" is.

I used to explain the distinction between praise and worship in church to children with a mandarin. I could praise the mandarin at great length for its brilliant orange colour, its transportability, its ease of storage, its skin that peeled off so easily, its segments that divided and enabled me to share the mandarin (the kids loved that part!), its health benefits and of course its amazing flavour. So I can praise a mandarin, just as I can list God's wonderful attributes and praise him. But to worship a mandarin is just silly. I would put a mandarin up on the front edge of the pulpit and then go down before it and bow to it, which caused great hilarity. The kids could see how stupid it was, and I hope you can too.

So we can follow and give thanks and praise to many things, but there is no point at which we should be worshipping mandarins, sports cars, houses, diamond rings, football stars, movie stars, politicians or anyone or anything but God alone. Worshipping anything else breaches the first and second commandments, and is simply foolish. Only God created the universe, only God rescued us in Jesus, only God gives us his Spirit. Therefore, uniquely, only God is worshipped.

So in church, **thanksgiving and piety are ABOUT US reacting to God, praise is ABOUT GOD, and true worship is addressed directly TO GOD**. Christian worship services should contain elements of praise, thanksgiving and piety, and these all should build around a core of true worship to provide a complete, enriching, engaging and uplifting experience that resonates within the soul of the worshipper and brings glory to God.

There is one other thing we need to say about what worship is. **Worship is costly**. What do I mean by that? Well, I'm not just talking about the offering, though of course giving is a part of worship too. But choosing to offer our lives to God, either in church or out of it, comes at a cost of another sort. To worship God and to live in service of him is a decision that precludes other choices. It means attending church instead of sleeping in on Sundays; it means sending the kids to Sunday School and not to sport; it means being filled with the Holy Spirit and not getting drunk on alcohol (Ephesians 5:18); it means valuing your family above yourself; it means nailing your colours to the mast at work and being prepared to be ridiculed for your faith; it means willing yourself to sing songs when you don't feel like it; it means reading from the Bible when nothing in it "jumps off the page" at you; it means accepting tasks that help the church function; it means being mature and compassionate toward those "extra-grace-required" people; it means exalting God when all the circumstances of your life might suggest that he is ignoring you; it means a commitment to be known as God's person wherever you are. It's taking up your cross and following. It's costly: but then, as King David put it, "I will not sacrifice to the Lord my God offerings that cost me nothing." (2 Samuel 24:24).

WHY WORSHIP?

Now that we have a better feel for what worship is, let's think briefly about why we worship. There are good reasons!

First, the desire to **worship is innate in us.** Being created by God and in his image has also given us an inbuilt desire for relationship with him. Some describe this as "a God-shaped hole" that needs filling. Worship fulfils this natural longing, and when we discover God as the proper object of our worship and put aside the other things we've tried, it becomes the most deeply satisfying activity in our world.

Secondly, **worship is a logical response** to the situation we find ourselves in. Any more than a moment's thought about where we are and how we came to be here quickly has us concluding we are the work of our creator God, a God so vast and extraordinary that the sensible response to him is worship. And that's before we get to the saving work of Jesus! Once we recognize our salvation then our desire to thank him and praise him is redoubled. And when we add the gift of the Holy Spirit to guide and shape our lives, the only logical way to respond to this treasure trove of blessing is worship.

We **worship also because God requires it**. It is his commandment that we worship him with heart, soul, mind and strength. If we choose to follow him then we obey this command willingly and wholeheartedly.

We also **worship to please God**—to put a smile on his face. God advises us to come to him with simple, pure hearts and motives, as young children might come to their parents with a happy, coloured, stick-figure drawing of them. Just as we smile when our children express love, so God smiles on us, and responds in loving ways. Don't ever think that you are too old, or too mature, or too sophisticated to come to God as a child. Compared to him, we are always little children who struggle to learn his ways and express our love appropriately.

And finally, as William Temple reminded us earlier, we **worship because God is constantly giving back to us as we do**. As we worship he surrounds us with his love, eases our burdens and cares, teaches us how to live, opens our hearts to his people and his mission, giving us a new focus in our living for him. His grace overflows upon us, he speaks to us, he heals us and he feeds us with nourishment for every aspect of our life.

WHAT SHOULD A WORSHIP SERVICE BE?

Because of what worship is, and because of our need to worship God together regularly, there are some things we can say about what a service of worship should seek to involve its participants in. Worship services are participatory. While there are elements of it that require our participation to be sitting and listening, a service is supposed to engage all its attendees all the time. Worship is our joint offering to God of all that is taking place.

From what we have said already, it is obvious that the primary intention for our corporate worship is for it to be **honouring to God**. The old catechism put it that "the chief end of man", the ultimate purpose of humankind, "is to glorify God, and enjoy him forever."[5] Our worship should encompass our adoration for the entire wonderful Trinity that we know as God—the Father, the Son and the Holy Spirit.

A service of worship should be an opportunity for God's people to **express love**, for God is love. We can, in worship, express love for God and for each other. We can bear one another's burdens, empathise with community pain and struggle, celebrate the joys of childbirth and marriage, weep with those who mourn, and in a thousand ways express love for each other as we pour out our hearts to God in love and gratitude for his love of us.

Worship should provide a **chance to learn** and develop maturity in faith and godly living. The reading and preaching of the Word is a crucial part of our growth together, and equips us for taking that Word to the world around us.

Worship should provide opportunity for the **fellowship of the saints**—a chance for God's people to interact and spark off each other. This happens when we sing and pray together, when we celebrate the sacraments together, and it's good if there are other moments in a service when we hear each other's stories and share our joys and sorrows.

---

[5] Westminster Shorter Catechism.

Worship should provide an opportunity for **giving**. While the whole service is our gift to God, our very life and everything that we have is a gift from him—on loan until we join him in the eternal Kingdom. In response to his giving nature, our love for God, his ways and his mission are wonderfully and tangibly expressed when we give materially out of what he has given us to advance his Kingdom on earth.

A service of worship should provide time for **ministry**. We are all broken people who come to the Great Physician for healing and wholeness. A church building is an interesting place. Almost always they are decorated—in various styles—to honour God, but I used to tell my congregations that it was as much a hospital as a temple. Our gatherings should always be a time for sharing our burdens with God and each other, and for praying for the sick and the emotionally and spiritually broken, and for declaring God's forgiveness and seeking his intervention.

Worship should seek to be **imaginative**. Made in the image of our Creator, we humans have been given a wonderful gift of creativity ourselves—and God anticipates that we will use it. When he tells us to "sing a new song to the Lord" (Psalm 96:1), it's because he knows we have the capacity to invent new songs. And our artistry and creative energy cover many fields of interest, from drama to dancing, from painting to processions and from clowning to coffee making.

God gave us five senses—sight, hearing, smell, touch and taste. Unsurprisingly, God has the capacity to engage with them all, so let's offer them—in part to thank him for the gift of them, and in part to stimulate God's people, many of whom respond to much more than the regular offerings of sound and sight that are produced for worship.

A worship service should be **refreshing**. God's people will worship him more truly, more completely and more joyously when they can say a hearty "Amen!" to what is being done through them, for them and by them. That means that worship will inevitably work best for its participants when it is culturally relevant—that is, that it recognises who they are and taps into that to release them in praise of their wonderful God. We will discuss this further shortly. Cultural relevance doesn't imply any lack of reverence, and it does ensure that what happens has a strong chance of resonating in the hearts of those present.

One last thing: worship should be offered as well as we can possibly manage. When a service is prepared and presented well it creates an enhanced opportunity for each of its participants to connect with and honour their Lord. Whatever talent may be available on a given day, we should seek to present everything to the very best of our ability. It should seek to be energizing and not draining; engaging and not boring.

WHAT HINDERS WORSHIP?

Just as doing things well enhances a worship experience, so also there are things that create barriers to worship—and I'm not just talking about whether you may like or dislike a particular worship style. I'm thinking of barriers like:

- **Fear**—while it is right to have a "fear" of God in the sense of a reverence and awe at his majesty and holiness, we should not be afraid of God—he is our loving heavenly Father who longs for us to come to him just as an earthly parent longs for their children to visit.
- **Shyness**—God sees and knows everything about us, which might be an embarrassing thought for some, but the point is that there is no reason to be shy before him.
- **Pride**—sometimes our reluctance to enter into worship is more about pride: not wanting to be in some way embarrassed before other people. Don't be proud when

you come to worship.

- **Feelings**—worship is an act of our will, but our feelings and emotions are very much a part of our humanity and belong in worship. Leaving yourself emotionally detached from worship will stifle it; letting your feelings take over will too. Be fully alive to worship, and fully aware in it.

- **Familiarity**—there is a comfort and security in routine, but when things are too predictable true worship is quickly hindered. And remember that "three songs and a prayer" can be just as boring a routine as always reading the same pages from a prayer book.

- **Selfishness**—it's not about you, whether you're the old minister who likes his hymns or the young enthusiast who wants the latest and greatest.

- **Stale relationship with God**—we all have times when God seems distant, but don't let your relationship with him go stale through a lack of prayer and time in his Word.

- **No relationship with God**—it's hard to worship a God you don't know. So find out who he is, and bring your heart to him.

So there are a number of reasons why an individual might hinder their own worship. But when the whole congregation has its worship hindered we need to try to recognise the causes and address them.

We have probably all attended services that have felt "flat". This happens for a lot of reasons. Maybe as a church you have reached a point where everything is predictable. Maybe your church has struggled to adjust musically to a changing congregation. Whatever the reason, I hope that the contents of this book will go a long way toward changing things for the better.

2 WHAT MAKES A SERVICE?

Now that we have some sort of idea about what worship is and what we are attempting to do when we worship together, we can turn our attention to the construction of a service of worship. Whether you are part of a conservative or traditional church and used to written liturgy, or a contemporary church with a freer worship style, you still have an order of service—it's just that one is a bit more obvious or detailed than the other.

In looking at what worship is we identified four different aspects of worship: thanksgiving, true worship, praise and piety. These intermingle a great deal, although to my mind they also start to make suggestions about how we might order a service.

The wonderful 100th Psalm tells us to enter his courts with thanksgiving, and that is often a great starting place for a service. We come to church each week because we are thankful to God and want to express that, so it suggests a way of starting a service.

After thanking and praising God and confessing our sins we are able to move into true worship, honouring God with all our hearts.

Praise we defined as talking about God, which makes me think of that part of a service where we listen to God's Word and hear it preached, because we are learning about God in those times.

Finally, piety is when we speak of our desire to follow God, and that calls to mind the end part of a service when we respond to God by committing ourselves to him anew and prepare to go into the world to share his love.

So, put very simply, there is a framework for a service in those four aspects of worship—thanksgiving, worship, praise and piety or, in terms of what we do, entering, worshipping, learning and responding. Most services, whether traditional or modern, follow this pattern on most occasions.

Within that broad, overall framework, the parts of a service are a bit like building blocks. You can put them together in various configurations and achieve a pleasing result. Not every service requires every element, but if we set out some possibilities then you will be able to assess what happens in your regular services (and why) and build from there according to what you discern to be a helpful approach for any given day.

Let's look at the building blocks of a service now. What should be in there? What does the Bible say happens when people worship God? The Bible describes many kinds of events in worship, from kneeling, bowing, falling down, raising hands, singing, shouting for joy, and dancing, to using musical instruments, telling stories, teaching and, of course, attitudes of humility and reverence.

I think the major building blocks are songs and other music, reading the Word, preaching, prayer, testimony, and Holy Communion. Interspersed with those are other important elements like fellowship, the offering and even the notices! We'll come to music soon and address it in great detail later, but first let's consider the others.

PRESENTING THE WORD

There is no more crucial aspect to Christian living than that it be anchored deep in the Word of God. And it's vital that we study the Word together, and explore its meaning regularly and consistently. If we expect God to speak into our lives and enlighten them, then the primary way that will happen is through the Bible.

Of course, we can read the Bible alone, and we should, every day. But on our own it's easy to get drawn in by one facet, or to focus only on those parts that are familiar or comforting. When we immerse ourselves in God's Word together, we benefit from each other, and from the trained wisdom of godly leaders and preachers who help us interpret the Word for our current world.

All through the Christian centuries church gatherings have been used to read the Scriptures and to preach the Word. It is vital that these continue!

In my view, **not every service has to have the Word read, or preached—but those times should be the rare exceptions**, not the rule. I have noted a current trend not to read the Scriptures, often simply allowing the preacher of the day to read those parts that he or she is referring to. It's not a practice that I'm completely happy with.

As a preacher, I know how easy it is to read some verses and not others, or to focus only on a small part of a passage as it supports the thrust of the message. My counter to that is to **have someone read from the Bible** whatever readings have been chosen for that day (whether you follow a lectionary or not) so that the people have the chance to hear the Word together unedited by the preacher or anyone else. This was often the practice in the days when few could read, and I believe it is still a healthy one. This reminds the people that they are united by God's Word, as well as reminding them of its content.

Today, of course, the Bible can be presented in different ways to good effect. There are several audio and even video versions of the Bible, or parts of it, that can be used to give the Scripture reading added impact. Likewise, a dramatic acting out of the verses of Scripture can add impact to its meaning. These are helpful and innovative ways of achieving the intent of bringing the gospel to the people in its purest form. These are probably best used for special occasions, as they might lose their impact if they become routine—as well as being a challenge logistically in most churches.

If reading the Word of God is vital, so too is expounding it. God's people—and **all who come to worship—need to hear how the Good News plays out in their world**, and how it can change their lives and give them new focus and purpose. There are huge possibilities for innovative delivery of a message these days, including drama, movie clips, poetry and satellite messages from other venues, but they are a rare exception to the norm. Over the long haul, there is no substitute for the spoken word of a living, breathing person who stands before the people and imparts God's Word through everyday language.

Presenting a sermon is an art in itself, and beyond the scope of this book. But the ground rules for me are that the message is biblically-based, that it is relevant to the lives of the listeners and that it is presented in a manner which is engaging for them. Long dissertations on the materials used to build the tabernacle are only valid insofar as they can be applied to the people who hear it. Equally, there is no place for long dissertations on the football Grand Final unless there are lessons to be learned which have a basis anchored firmly in the Bible. In either case, there is the potential to have substantial numbers of the hearers "switch off" at some point. The first commandment of preaching is, "Thou shalt not be boring."

Whatever else is being presented in a given service, it is almost certain that **the Word will be the controlling element. It will set the theme for the day**. It will affect the music that is selected; it will affect the style and length of other components of the service.

If you are planning the service but you are not the preacher, it is crucial to the overall direction—and the effect—of the service that you speak with the person who is preaching and gain a good grasp of the message and supporting Bible passages, so that you can construct the service appropriately. Without this input, what happens in your service is truly in the hands of God! And, while I trust him completely to make use of all our offerings, he has also given us gifts, skills and brains to use, and when we use those for him I am certain of his pleasure at the end result.

THE PRAYERS OF THE PEOPLE

If the Word is vital in hearing God speak to us, then prayer is a vital part of us speaking back. While all of our lives are prayers to God, those times when we stop and speak directly to him are surely blessed and important windows into the heart of God.

Whether we take time to craft a prayer with measured words written down that carefully state our thinking, or we pour out our words in a spontaneous reflection of our hearts at that moment, prayer is an opportunity to tell God what concerns us and to have him take note of the desires of his people.

In more formal services of worship, prayers are offered at a number of points, covering such topics as praise and adoration of God, thanksgiving, prayers that dedicate offerings, prayers of confession, and prayers that seek God's intervention in human affairs (known as supplications or intercessions). In more modern services, these are often reduced to two or three, with a combined adoration/confession/thanksgiving prayer, and a prayer of intercession. Frequently a prayer is offered to dedicate the offering, but not always.

There seems to be a trend at the moment toward very minimal prayer content in worship. It's not a trend I'm too happy about! If anything, **I would rather err in the direction of too much prayer** (can there ever be too much?) than not enough. Some academics have argued that prayer is a personal communication with God and that there is no place for public prayer at all. It might be an interesting debate intellectually, but it is one that is ruled irrelevant by the fact that public prayer has been part of the church from its very inception, and continues to be so, regardless of any academic's view to the contrary.

One area where more traditional forms of worship have lacked is in the area of prayer for healing. Those prayers, if offered, were often part of a special "healing service" held perhaps once a quarter or less. The modern trend, which I applaud, is to offer prayer for healing at every service—usually at the conclusion. I believe this approach more accurately reflects Jesus' healing ministry, and underlines the caring role of the church.

Another modern trend with prayer is to have a musician play quietly as the prayer is offered. This can be truly effective and I have seen it used extremely well in quite a number of circumstances. But be aware that it can also be a distraction if done poorly. If the music is too loud, or too bright—bouncy, fast and happy—then it quickly overpowers the spoken prayer. It's also a potential distraction if a familiar melody is played. People start humming the song or thinking its words instead of praying the prayer.

The other helpful and powerful ingredient to prayer is one that is often feared and seldom used: **silence**. We so rarely offer room for God to talk back! In periods of silence congregants are able to commune with God directly, to amplify any points of the spoken prayer that have personal implications, and to listen for the voice of God in reply. Yet we are fearful of silence.

On radio, when nothing is being said, a silence is odd. Technicians call it "dead air". And often in church we feel the same: that if something isn't being said or done in any given instant, that time is somehow wasted. In using silence, it is best to explain it beforehand, so that people are aware they will have space to fill by themselves.

IS THERE A WITNESS?

There is one element of worship which is frequently missing from services—both traditional and modern—and I can only think that the devil discourages it specifically because of its great power. That element is testimony. Jesus told us that we would be his witnesses "in all Judea and Samaria, and to the ends of the earth." (Acts 1:8). This verse is, of course, about evangelism, and is almost universally thought of as the "out there" part of Christianity. And yet the power of a conversion story told in a church can do several things at once: it can enliven the faith of the other believers; it can speak to any not-yet-believers who are present; and it can bring great glory to God.

I have always sought to include the power of personal stories in services of worship. This can happen in a number of ways, from allowing a person time to tell a lengthy testimony (perhaps even as the sermon for the day), to hearing of the work of para-church organisations like Gideons, World Vision or Compassion, hearing the reports of returning missionaries, to simply allowing a time when people can step forward to tell briefly of an event from the past week.

Probably the most powerful stories I've heard have come from people in the congregation—often not the usual up-front ones—who have been able to describe the work of God in their life simply and in a way that people understand and can relate to.

These **testimonies help God's people to recognise and appreciate God at work in their own context**. They are a cause for praise and celebration, and prompt people to worship God and thank him for his goodness. They lift the faith level of the whole church.

Prophecy often has a similar impact—and, yes—there will be prophets in your church—prophecy is one of the gifts of the Spirit that is given so that the church can function. In these days many churches are unused to receiving prophecy or trusting their prophets, and this trust takes time to build. But when a prophet is identified and has proven trustworthy, their additions to worship raise faith, bring glory to God and help to point the way for the church—particularly toward worship. In my experience, prophets encourage greater love for God, and reiterate God's love for us, in a way that inspires greater devotion.

HOLY COMMUNION

To try and summarize Holy Communion in a few words is like trying to fit an elephant in a Coke bottle, but I'll give it a go.

Holy Communion is a sacrament. What is a sacrament? A sacrament is "an outward and visible sign of an inward and spiritual grace".[6] In other words, it's a symbolic action that we take, that we were told to do by Jesus, that provides a visible sign of, and invokes, an outpouring of God's love and undeserved favour, and that assures us of his continued presence in our lives.

A sacrament has two essential components: the *grace* of God, and the *faith* of the recipient. God pours his grace upon us in the sacraments, but *unless we receive them in faith*, they are, to unbelieving eyes, just so much water poured on someone's head, or a mystifying dunking of someone in a pool or river, or a very strange snack of bread and wine. With faith they become blessed and sacred moments when God speaks to us in profound and marvellous ways.

With Holy Communion (called the Eucharist or the Lord's Supper in some traditions) we repeat and remember what Jesus did on the night of his betrayal and take bread and wine from him as his disciples did, reminding ourselves that Christ bore our sins through his death in our place. Through the taking of the elements we align ourselves anew with him and draw faith and strength for life's journey through his grace.

Every church takes its celebration of the sacrament of Holy Communion very seriously, yet their understandings and practices can vary significantly. I am not seeking to venture into those areas in what I say, and I am not writing to debate the merits of transubstantiation or any other doctrine relating to church belief and practice. I urge you to consult with your pastor/minister/priest on the proper conduct of the sacrament according to your rites and traditions, many of which require the presence and participation of an ordained person. My comments are designed to help. Where they draw your criticism, I can only advise you to refer to your own

---

6 'The Catechism', *An Australian Prayer Book* (1978), Anglican Information Office Press, Sydney.

church's theology and doctrines to establish your own proper practice.

Many denominational churches have quite set liturgies for the conduct of Communion, and where that is the practice of your church, I advise you to follow them. But churches that are more free-flowing, including house churches and some small, lay-led congregations, often have no set pattern for the conduct of Communion, so what I say here I hope will be of assistance in those cases, and you can add it to your own understanding and other research.

Communion becomes almost a service within a service, as there are certain things that should happen to sustain the integrity, reverence and power of the sacrament:

a. There should be an **introduction** that underlines the importance of what is done. This could take all day if we were to try and cover it completely, so an aspect of the meaning, purpose and value of Communion is focussed upon, with a different highlight next time.

b. There should be a **prayer, confessing our sins and thanking God** for his forgiveness, and honouring his majesty and faithfulness.

c. There should be a **rehearsal of the events of the Last Supper**, explaining Jesus' inauguration of the sacrament, based on Scripture (one of the four Gospel accounts or Paul's reference in 1 Cor. 11).

d. There should be **a prayer asking God, by his grace, to set apart the elements to be used** (the bread and wine/grape juice) for his holy purpose, that as we receive them in faith they would become the body and blood of Christ for us.

e. The **elements should then be distributed** and consumed reverently.

f. Finally, there should be **a concluding prayer** thanking God and asking his help with living out the meaning of what has been done.

Various parts of the above liturgy are sung in some traditions, while the use of appropriate music often adds immeasurably to the moment.

As to methods of distribution, there are many that are possible: from individual cups and cut bread or wafers, to a common cup and common loaf with portions broken from it for serving. Some people are wary of the common cup for hygiene reasons. Another common practice is to take the piece of bread and dip it in the cup, thus receiving both elements at once. The people can receive the elements where they sit, or come forward and receive them at a distribution point or points, perhaps choosing to kneel if they are physically able.

Choosing the elements for a Communion service should be done thoughtfully. There are many possibilities, including a large loaf, cut bread, wafers, unleavened bread and so on. Some denominations use alcoholic wine, while others, cautious for those who have problems with alcohol, use grape juice. Some churches offer both alternatives. The wine/juice should be red in colour, to help identify it with Jesus' blood.

I have witnessed other common foods used in the sacrament, such as chocolate biscuits and Coca-Cola offered in a youth camp setting, but I counsel against those, even though they were justified at the time as being "culturally relevant". I think we should plan ahead sufficiently to use appropriate foods to retain the historicity, credibility and reverence of what we do.

The frequency of Communion varies from occurring in every service in some denominations to as rarely as four times a year in others. There is no rule about it, and biblical references are offered to justify different stances. Often the deciding factor revolves around its impact on visitors and how they can feel "left out", finding the ritual strange. My denomination settled on once per month, and I have become comfortable with that, as it offers the sacrament frequently without having it too predominant for visitors and inquirers. You should adhere to the practice of your denomination. If your church is an independent one, then discuss the matter and resolve it according to your joint leading from the Spirit.

THE OFFERING

All churches need funding. They need to fund their mission, pay for their buildings or their rent, pay their staff and contribute to the world generally. Collecting money for these purposes has always been problematic as Christians in worship are usually trying to take their focus off material things and put it onto spiritual ones. And yet, **using the resources we are blessed with wisely and for godly purposes is at the heart of the gospel**. So we shouldn't feel too squeamish about the fact that we need money to function properly.

Where to schedule an offering within a service often has people scratching their heads, to the point where I have attended churches where there is no offering—members are instead expected to remember to place their gift in a receptacle at the back after the service is completed. This is OK if people remember, but it does tend to disenfranchise visitors and others who don't know the system, and those with poor memories! There also may be no physical collection due to online giving. However, communication about the offering will still need to happen at some point.

There are two logical times during a service when an offering might be taken: first, during the period when we are focussed upon God, when our offerings are part of our worship of him; and second, as part of the period after the hearing of the Word read and preached, when we are responding and our gifts form part of that response.

Stories circulate that when a challenging message has been delivered that might irritate some members there is a fall in the level of giving! I cannot corroborate them from personal experience, but the very existence of the stories has me favouring the former time, during worship. That way, a preacher can deliver the message God has placed on their heart without fear of affecting the income!

Special giving also needs consideration. There are frequent calls upon the church to support missionaries, welfare organisations and special projects, while as Christians we desire to join in the community's giving to special appeals for natural disasters and other events. These can be handled by way of special envelopes to separate the donations from other church income, or by placing an offering bowl near the door for a "retiring offering". A separate collection could also be made during the service at the time of focussing on the special need.

FELLOWSHIP

The wonderful fellowship of God's people overflows before and after services as folk greet each other and catch up on important issues of ministry and caring. I believe there is a place within the service for the fellowship of the Holy Spirit to flow too. Often visitors or first-time attendees will leave before the morning tea, so it's good to have a chance to welcome each other in the context of worship and before they miss out on the love of the people.

This can be done more formally, with a "passing of the peace" where one will say, "The peace of the Lord be with you," while the other responds, "And also with you." Or there can simply be an invitation to greet one another casually at a suitable point in the service—perhaps during the offering or while the children depart for Sunday School, if that is your practice.

The notices form another moment when the fellowship of the church is, or can be, emphasised. Plan this time into your service where you feel the need for a "break"—a change in mood, intensity, or just to allow people to refocus for the next part of the service. Some churches leave the notices until right near the end, so the notices are remembered and there is no interruption to the service. That can work, but it might also mean that the message of the sermon and the theme of the service get diluted with relatively unimportant matters, just when you want to send the people out full of hope, or embracing a challenge.

THE ROLE OF MUSIC

Music is powerful. If you need any convincing of that fact, just think how often advertisers use it to promote their products on TV and radio. Right now you could probably sing the jingles of half a dozen commercials.

It is also an all-pervading element of modern society, with powerful influence on the young. Kids these days have grown up with music entertaining and teaching them from birth. Our young people can be subjected to influences from Play School and the Wiggles to Madonna and the Sex Pistols.

The joy for Christians is that music also has a great capacity to link the truth of God's Word with its pitch, tone, rhythm, rhyme and repetition to embed in our hearts and minds verses of Scripture and the salvation story of Jesus Christ. Just as advertisers and rock stars use its power, so too the church has for centuries sought to **use music to honour God and to teach the precepts of the faith** to young and old alike.

There was a time when church music was pure—and then

some radical upstart introduced a new-fangled instrument called an organ and messed it all up! But seriously, down the ages the church has used music in countless forms, from the "psalms, hymns and spiritual songs" (Ephesians 5:19) of biblical times, to chants, choirs, orchestras, organs and just about every instrument ever invented. One country congregation I served boasted piano accordion and banjo! I loved it.

Modern Christian songs tend to mirror the style of today's music. That means that they probably appeal most to those in their mid-twenties to mid-thirties, because they are largely the ones writing it. The younger ones tend not to have developed the skill to write well, and anyone older than mid-thirties has tended to drop off the cutting edge of modern music, as they raise their families and become more deeply embroiled in their "day jobs".

This is not new, of course. Our now "dated" hymns were once the powerful new songs of their day, borrowing heavily from the popular tunes and music styles of their time. **Over time the music of the church gently gets sifted**, and the least helpful ones drop off the play-list once they have lost their freshness. The hymns we are left with today are probably the best ten percent of what was produced at the time. This same sifting process has not yet occurred for many modern songs, which are sung for their popularity as much as their helpful content or musical quality. All of which is OK. But I am saying that you can—and should—be selective in what you use and why, whether it's old or new.

Music is crucial to worship because of its power to teach, its engaging quality, and of course because it is **the primary participatory element of worship**. The point when we stand to sing together is the key moment at which the people of God can open up and collectively state their faith and unite as one in their worship of God. From my observation, no matter how good the preaching or other elements of a service may have been, people go home most refreshed, most satisfied, most rewarded for their attendance, when they have "had a good sing", as my Dad used to put it.

Therefore (as Paul often says!) don't ever underestimate the importance of music. Whether it's traditional or modern, good music—chosen, led and performed to the peak of your ability—can take your people to the very throne room of God.

3 BEFORE YOU START...

Having considered the various elements that might make up a service, we need to think about what we are trying to achieve with our service design. First and foremost is that we are worshipping God. As one writer puts it,

> *The dominant mood of the occasion must not be that of a lot of needy people desperate for help and health, but of the reality of God, the Father, Son and Holy Spirit, in whose hands we all find ourselves.*[7]

And our desire is to enable a particular group of Christians and seekers to come together to immerse themselves in the grace and love of our triune God. So, for any given service, it seems to me that we intend a service to be godly in its focus; to be truly Christian in its content; to suit the congregation it is prepared for; to pursue its theme successfully; and to have a smooth, logical progression that integrates the various parts into a meaningful whole.

For a service to suit its congregation we need to think about that congregation. Its smooth and logical progression comes from what I think of as "flow". Successfully pursuing a theme is not just about deciding upon one but ensuring the various

---

[7] Richard G Jones, *Groundwork of Worship and Preaching* (1980), Epworth, London, p153.

parts contribute to it. And its godly focus and Christian content depend upon the theology that is promoted by what is done. Let's start to explore those issues now.

WHAT TYPE AND STYLE?

When you think about the people who will attend the service there are a number of issues that arise instantly. The first is, what type of service are you preparing?

Funerals, weddings, ordination or induction services are all designed specifically to address those occasions and are beyond the scope of this book, except in very general terms, as are occasions like a baptism at the beach or a community service after a disaster. Services at a nursing or retirement home also require some thinking outside the normal run of what is possible and helpful for a Sunday morning. Services such as those for youth or healing or an anniversary are services that fit our general approach more closely but will require some adjustment to fit the congregation and the circumstances.

The style of a service could be anything, ranging from youth, arty, edgy, café, dramatic, to ultra-traditional, complete with pageantry. This book focuses on normal Sunday services, so when you apply the principles of this book to those wider types and styles you will stay consistent and strong in what you present.

CULTURE: WHAT IS YOUR CHURCH LIKE?

Before you plan a service, you need to take account of your church's culture. What does that mean? Well, of course I am initially referring to the culture of the society that surrounds the church. The type of society that the church finds itself in will have a bearing on the type of worship that "works" there.

A service somewhere in the Pacific will have the cultural impact of its Polynesian attendees—as will services of the Copts in Egypt, or Russian farmers in Siberia. Western culture pervades services in many parts of Australia; though in some parts of the country, services are shaped by the large numbers of Indigenous Australians, and in others, by large numbers of people from all over the globe. And even in western cultures, there are differences between Australian western culture and British, American, Swedish or German western culture.

If you are preparing a service for Australians, it needs to "feel" Australian for the congregation to relate. This might mean utilising our dry sense of humour as well as ideas like "giving everyone a fair go", and so on. And once the church's general culture is established, there is need to sharpen the cultural focus still further, onto the culture that is particular to your church. Is your church in the city or the country? Is it large or small? Does it have a long history or very little? Are they mostly people who were born in Australia or more recent arrivals? What is its spiritual and theological heritage? Is it made up of younger people or older people? How are children included? Are there any children? What time is the service to be held? Will the preacher survive if he or she speaks for more than twenty minutes? Or less than forty?

But there is more. There is also your church's worship culture. Every church develops its own culture for worship, and that culture gets learned and ingrained over time. Are there always three songs and then a prayer? Has it become the practice only to use songs or hymns from a particular book? Which version of the Lord's Prayer is used? Is it used at all? Does the same person always read the notices? Would there be heart-attacks if drums were used? If drums were NOT used?

Some churches have existed for decades or even centuries and worshipped in a particular style, governed in part by its people's heritage and probably in part by its buildings and equipment. If you have a building with a pipe organ and choir stalls, then the building is saying something about the kind of worship that it was built for and has been common there. If there is dust on the organ, a drum kit and a row of microphone and guitar stands, there has been some change to the old format. Do you have a cross on the wall? Or is there a tiny gold cross on the table that is dominated by a rank of organ pipes behind it? If you move the cross or take it away, what message will the people receive?

People learn to worship in particular ways, and can be upset when changes are made. This is where the "war" of the music comes in. It's not that old people like hymns and young ones prefer songs. There are plenty of examples of older folk enjoying modern worship and vice versa. **It's more about what sort of music and worship was happening at the time when the particular attendee felt most "alive" in church; when their faith was at some kind of peak.** For many people this experience comes at the time of conversion or deepened commitment, and whatever type of worship was present when that internal journey was at its most profound, whether they were younger or older at the time, is the sort of worship they will always tend to think is "best", or at least their favourite.

In your church you may have folk whose "moment" came at a Billy Graham Crusade. They will love you forever if you play "How Great Thou Art" and "Just as I am". Older folk have probably had their best moments with the hymns of Charles Wesley, Isaac Watts and Fanny Crosby. There will be a group from the 1970s whose favourite song is Jack Hayford's "Majesty". In the 1980s it was Graham Kendrick and "Shine Jesus Shine", in the 1990s it was Darlene Zschech's "Shout to the Lord" and songs by Geoff Bullock, and in the last ten years it's been Matt Redman and Reuben Morgan. People respond instantly and emotionally to the songs from the time of their moment. Remember earlier when we talked about the power of music?

This is why the arguments over music styles often get so vehement. It's not about oldies versus youngies; it's about whether you are providing (or taking away) a style of worship in which a group of people have their personal best experiences and memories of what it means to worship, and therefore the style of worship they have most invested in emotionally and spiritually.

So the worship culture of your church will have grown through and because of these influences and their combined effect on the congregation. Your service style might ultimately be set by the majority opinion as to what style of worship they favour. Or it might be set by a church council, or a smaller group who tend to run things. Or it might have become the priest/pastor/minister's prerogative. But whoever does it, it will take into account all that history.

Whatever influences have determined the worship culture, there will be a sizeable inertia to overcome if it is to be altered. As I said, people have learned to worship that way and have become comfortable with it, so changing it—even just to vary it at times—requires skill, tact and time. Remember the old adage about change says that 15% will adopt the change immediately and love it; the next 35% will adopt it relatively soon; the next 35% will, over time, eventually adopt it, and the last 15% will probably never adopt it.

Don't feel that everything you do has to be new, or involve change. **Successful worship design is more about you being "in tune" with the church** than your ability or desire to change things.

So what I mean by endeavouring to make your services **"culturally relevant" is threefold: it is taking account of the surrounding culture of society, the particular culture**

of your church's situation, and the learned worship culture of the congregation.

I wouldn't want you to think that your church's culture is some kind of unyielding straitjacket: once you know about it and prepare within it (or at least recognise it) you can bring a whole new light and shade to worship. I believe that with careful attention to the construction of each service, embracing subtle shifts in content and design week by week, the congregation can not only become less "set-in-its-ways" but also can begin to enjoy and thrive on the variety. And if a certain person or group did not enjoy what happened on a particular occasion, at least they have the reassurance that next week will probably be different!

FLOW: SMOOTHING OUT THE BUMPS

A service of worship at its best will have a flow, a sense of smooth, internal integrity—almost a rhythm. You see, a service takes its attendees on a journey. It gathers people, allows them to praise and worship God, allows them to hear God's word read and preached, and allows them to respond to it, leaving the worship experience feeling refreshed or challenged for the week ahead and in tune with God and his people. How these things are attained can vary enormously, but one of the secrets to a satisfying service is to achieve a smooth flow from element to element. Some of it is simple logic, but at its best it's more than that.

Logically, certain things should happen in a certain order, and that's a good start. But **real "flow" is achieved when there is a feeling, a sense of "rightness" about how things happen that is so natural that you almost don't notice the transitions.** You come out really refreshed and satisfied, like you would if you had seen a really good movie, or theatre production, opera or ballet. Of course, most of your refreshing and satisfaction is the work of the Holy Spirit, but when a service is well ordered and "flowing" many souls respond and open more to the work of the Spirit: **the flow of the service is a catalyst that helps your attendees to open up to God and allow him to work in them**.

This is one of the major reasons why I recommend that worship be "culturally relevant". A service that is in tune with its attendees culturally, and achieves a good level of flow in delivering its message, will open more people to God's Spirit than one where the people have no real understanding of, or relationship to, what is happening.

Before you conclude each service plan you should be asking yourself (or your team) whether what you have prepared has created smooth pathways by which people will come into God's presence, will be inspired to move spiritually into worship, will be positioned well intellectually and emotionally to be taught from the Word, and will be released to be better followers of Jesus.

So as you plan you'll be asking yourself questions like, "What are the songs/hymns that I need to achieve a "flow" from the outside hustle to a place of focus on God? How can we transition from a moment of high praise to one of learning, or confession? How can this prayer serve to help people respond to what has been preached? What is the best means of sending the people out with joy in their hearts and a spring in their step, or with a determination to take up the challenge that is to be put to them and go for it?" All these questions and many others like them, when answered well, will help to produce "flow".

DIRECTION: WHERE IS IT ALL HEADED?

A service also has a direction. The **direction is about the theme of the worship** but is also linked to the ideas of entering, worshipping, learning and responding, and how that theme is introduced and embraced as each phase of the service progresses.

The **complication** that arises with direction is that every song, every prayer, every announcement, every movie clip— **every element of the service—has its own direction**. For example, a prayer that has as its main component a cry for those suffering floods in Bangladesh could be something of a distraction in a service about inner healing. A hymn or song whose final verse leads you on a triumphal march into heaven will probably not lead into a sermon about the brokenness of the drug trade. They're all good directions to go in, but become difficult to link together in one service. If you've just had a deep and meaningful time of worship and prayer ministry, it might not be the best moment to boisterously announce the barbecue after church.

So when you are planning how your service will deliver its theme and achieve "flow" you also need to be mindful of the direction of the various aspects of the service, and whether they work with, or against, the overall direction you want the service to move in, or even what you are trying to achieve at that point within the service.

You probably won't achieve a "flowing, directional" service for every situation. Ultimately there are too many aspects of a service that you have little input to or control over. Don't worry—that's where God really shines, and constantly surprises with the way in which he takes hold of what we have prepared and "tweaks" it to bring about just what he wants.

But I do hope that from reading this material you will start to look for the flow and direction yourself in what you prepare. This is not a mechanical process, but a living one. I hope you will **learn to "feel" what works and what doesn't, what is helpful and what isn't, what warms the heart and what doesn't.** Achieving this will not just be a matter of studying the various parts of a service and plugging them together in sequence, but looking deeper into the words and tunes of the hymns or songs, the content of the prayers, and the way in which various aspects of the service are conducted.

THEOLOGY: WHAT WILL YOUR SERVICE SAY?

OK, I don't want to trample on your beliefs as an individual or as a church. This is not a theology book in the sense that it is not trying to establish or defend a particular view of the Christian faith (although it probably does... read on!).

I read a prayer guide to Handel's "Messiah" recently which along the way also told me that the key focus of the gospel was social justice and that Christians, Jews and Muslims all worshipped the same God. Hmmm. I don't think it was the author's deliberate intention to impart these things; it was just that what he believed came through in his writings on an entirely different subject.

So I need to set this out to give you somewhere to turn to quickly so you can check what you're doing with your worship. You see, in the same way that everything you include has a direction, **every time you choose a hymn, or write a prayer, or suggest a song, or put up a banner, you are expressing theology** through it. The service you prepare WILL make theological statements, and **you need to understand enough theology so that the service you produce will be truly Christian** in what it says. **This isn't hard—but it is really important**. The power of music can attach itself to misleading theology, a "clever" movie clip can put the focus wrongly, and even a few stray words can create an unfortunate and incorrect impression of the gospel.

Apparently they teach bank staff to find counterfeit banknotes by having them study the real ones carefully—then the forgeries are easier to spot. So using the same principle, if we set out a simple, accurate description of the essence of Christianity, and you keep it in mind as you prepare your service, then counterfeit worship will be kept at bay too.

So what are **the essential tenets of Christianity**? We're not talking about the small areas of the faith that might separate Christians into Anglican, Baptist, Pentecostal or Uniting Churches. These are the things that are at the very core of Christian belief; the things we can all say a hearty "Amen" to.

I can think of two ways to approach this, so let's use both! The first is to remind ourselves of our core beliefs through the **Apostles' Creed**:

> *I believe in God, the Father almighty,*
> *Creator of heaven and earth,*
> *and in Jesus Christ, his only Son, our Lord,*
> *who was conceived by the Holy Spirit,*
> *born of the Virgin Mary,*
> *suffered under Pontius Pilate,*
> *was crucified, died and was buried;*
> *he descended into hell;*
> *on the third day he rose again from the dead;*
> *he ascended into heaven,*
> *and is seated at the right hand of God the Father almighty;*
> *from there he will come to judge the living and the dead.*
> *I believe in the Holy Spirit,*
> *the holy Christian Church,*
> *the communion of saints,*
> *the forgiveness of sins,*
> *the resurrection of the body,*
> *and the life everlasting. Amen.*[8]

---

[8] Although many English translations of the Apostles' Creed render this as "the holy catholic Church" (catholic meaning "universal" rather than Roman Catholic), here Christian has been substituted to avoid confusion.

This Creed has been recited as a true summation of our faith for centuries. It was composed in large part to deal with the very issue we are considering: that of people getting a bit off track.

The second way to deal with this is to express the same kind of thing in terms of the way it affects our modern thinking and life choices. I guess it might be called a statement of the **Christian "worldview"**—the kind of thinking and approach to life that is set up by our core beliefs and the impact of those beliefs on how we live life. Let's list some things here:

1. **God created the universe** and everything in it, including mankind in his image. Nothing "just happened".
2. **We chose to disobey** God and fell into sin.
3. Throughout the history of the Old Testament, people proved incapable of keeping a covenant: **there was—and is—no way to earn our redemption.**
4. **God sent his only Son** to teach us how to live, to show us God's love in tangible ways, **to die in our place and to conquer death** by rising from the grave.
5. Because of that, **Jesus Christ, the Son of God, our Saviour, is the only way to the Father**—there is no possible alternative.
6. **God sent the Holy Spirit to empower** his people (the Church) in spreading the Good News and doing the work of the Kingdom.
7. Our home is not here—we are foreigners on earth, and **our true home is in the heavenly Kingdom**, which we will enter when Christ comes again in power to judge the world and gather his people.
8. **Death is not the end** but a transition in our eternal life.
9. **We inherit his Kingdom as a free gift from God**

when we confess our sins, ask Jesus to be Lord of our lives and invite the Holy Spirit to dwell within us.

10. The **Bible is God's utterly trustworthy manual** for living and the final authority on earth for Christian faith.

11. **We worship one God in three persons**—the Father, the Son and the Holy Spirit.

12. **God's command is that we worship him alone, with heart, soul, mind and strength.** There is no room for other gods, whatever shape they come in.

13. **Jesus commands us to love our neighbours as ourselves.** There is no-one who is beyond redemption.

14. **God's will is for us to grow** more and more like Jesus Christ.

15. Having come to faith, **we serve Jesus in the building of his Kingdom here on earth** until he calls us home.[9]

So there it is. OK, I know that all sounds so simple it almost seems stupid to write it down, but within the Creed and those Christian worldview statements there is a test that you can use to determine what is helpful to Christian worship and what isn't. If someone suggests a nice song that leaves room for some other God to be worshipped, you will know immediately that it fails the test. If someone says talking about sin isn't cool and we don't really need to confess anyway, then they are straying from what the Christian faith teaches. If someone suggests a hymn all about Mother Nature, it is off track and needs amending or rejecting. If someone suggests a

---

[9] This list originally came from Rick Warren (Saddleback Church, Los Angeles, USA) but I have modified it over the years and cannot honestly say how much of it remains his or is now mine. Perhaps it is best if I gratefully acknowledge Rick as a source, and accept any criticism for errors, omissions and problems myself!

reading from the Koran it fails the test. If an artist includes a yin-yang symbol as part of a display, it fails the test. If someone prepares a prayer that suggests we can somehow earn our way to heaven through doing good deeds, we know it is off track and needs rewording.

Those statements summarize **where we are coming from as Christians.** When you keep your music choices, your prayers, your faith statements, your testimonies, your creative elements and your sermons within these parameters **you can have confidence that your service is "mainstream" Christian** and worthy of your people.

PREPARING THE HEART AND MIND

Finally, before you set out to construct a service of worship, it's crucial that you get your own heart, soul and mind in order. Remember that **everything you do is for the glory of God and in worship of him** (regardless of the setting you find yourself in) and that therefore it should be done to the very best of your ability. Planning a service of worship will take time, brain power, research, consultation and decision-making. Make sure you are ready to give the processes the time and effort they need.

The other **crucial thing to do before you start to plan a service is to pray.** Pray for your construction of the service, for all the people involved in presenting it, for the music elements that you choose, for the rehearsals, for your part in the service, for the technical stuff, for everyone and every part of what you are doing. If you are a team, pray together before you do anything else. If you are preparing on your own, spend the first part of your time deep in prayer: **open your heart to the Lord and your mind to his ways.**

4 PLANNING A SERVICE

Now that we know what might be in a service and what we are hoping to achieve, let's think about how to plan one. What comes first? What comes last? What "works" and what doesn't?

We have already referred briefly to the ordering of a service when we mentioned entering, worshipping, learning and responding in talking about flow and direction. But we have also seen that there are a number of other objectives for a service—fellowship, giving, healing prayer and so on, so we need to devise a plan that works for all the elements we need to include for a particular occasion, and produces a time of worship that has integrity, flow and direction around its theme and purpose.

Entering and leaving are obvious as beginning and end, but what to do in the middle? And with what do we begin and end? Let's look at a generic shape for a worship service now.

A GENERIC SHAPE FOR WORSHIP

The journey into the service needs to recognise that everyone is coming in from their routine lives. Some will be happy, some sad. Some will have had an argument on the way! **Your service needs to find a way to unite the people and get their attention onto the worship of God**. This could happen through a rousing praise song, a grand hymn, a drum roll and a reading from Scripture, and countless other variations, but they will all have a means of drawing people's attention into worship and away from what has been happening in their lives.

Psalm 100 tells us to enter his gates with thanksgiving and his courts with praise (Psalm 100:4). This describes entering the temple grounds, still somewhat distant from the holiest places. Songs and other elements that pick up on the ideas of **thanksgiving and praise** will be helpful ways into your service.

How long you take over this entering period will vary. From there, it is usually helpful to **move toward more exuberant praise or deeper worship.** This can come through further music, prayer and other carefully worded contributions that develop the mood of worship.

Before you go too far, however, **it's good to confess**. Confession and worship are very closely related. The nearer we come to God, the more conscious we are of our own shortcomings. Conversely, until we have dealt with our sin, it is difficult (impossible?) to come near to God, as Isaiah experienced (Isaiah 6:5). A time of confession can be a prayer, or a song, a prayer from a book, a solo song, a drama or whatever, but its point will be to engage the congregation in an act of confession.

Once hearts are set free, **true worship** is more probable, so try and design an opportunity for it. It might be aided by testimony, an offering, prayer and music, but try to allow time for the Spirit of God to move and open people's hearts.

After this, your people are ready for the other deep acts of learning and faith. This would be a good time for the **sacraments** of Holy Communion or Baptism. If not, then it is most logical and beneficial to head into the moments of the service that require true hearts aligned with the Spirit, like **intercessory prayer** and interactions with **the Word of God** through reading and preaching.

How to provide an opportunity for response in people to the Word in the way they live their lives is always a challenge. As James put it, we don't want to have just hearers of the Word but also those who put it into practice (James 2:26). **Before the service ends, it is good to allow people to respond in some meaningful way.** This might be achieved through prayer, an "altar call", standing in commitment, filling out a response card, an offering, a sacrament and many other ways, of course including music with lyrics that reinforce the Word and prompt people to go out into the world eager to follow the gospel anew. Songs of piety work especially well in this context, as people are encouraged to "own" what they have been part of, and to take it with them into their lives.

As you read this you might think, "well yes, that's all fine—it sounds like what we often do". If so, that's great: it means that there is at least a logical flow to the services that you are commonly part of. And now you know why it has been constructed in that way: it was not an accident. Apart from following the inherited traditions for worship in the church, what you have been doing is both logical and helpful.

But believe me, **mistakes are common**. Sometimes there are glaring problems, like prayers of confession that become intercession, songs that send people out placed at the beginning, great moments of worship destroyed by announcements, and so on. You can probably all think of one.

And of course I am not just talking about correcting a glaring error but improving a "good" service into a better one. This is not just about the mechanics of placing things in the "right" order. **There is no complete, consistent "right" order**, with a few exceptions, like coming in before you go out. I'm getting back to those questions of flow and direction. To achieve those things, it becomes a matter of paying attention to the detail of what is being said at which parts of the service, whether in song or prayer, in announcement or video clip.

Let me offer a practical example at this point. A service I attended a few years ago was a bit "scrambled" in its flow and direction. The minister was in the midst of a sermon series on prayer, and that week he decided to preach on praying for the sick. But also in the service he conducted an infant baptism, and had a discussion with a missionary family who were home on furlough.

The service started with a hymn and then we went into the baptism—it is common to conduct infant baptisms early in the service in case the child becomes unsettled. Then there was a worship time, a children's address (on kids helping their friends), an intercessory prayer, the sermon on healing the sick, the notices, the discussion with the missionary family, the offering and then a final song.

So, from my memory of it, the order was:

> Hymn
> Prayer of adoration
> Baptism
> 3 songs of worship
> Children's address
> Prayer for others and the world
> Sermon on prayer for the sick
> Announcements
> Talk with missionaries
> Offering
> Song
> Benediction

Can you see how the congregation's attention was dragged all over the place in that service? From newborn kids and baptism, to worship, to teaching kids to help their mates, to praying for the world, to learning about praying for the sick, to missionary work in a foreign country, and finally to giving.

How might it be made more flowing and better directed? My first suggestion would be to the preacher, suggesting that he vary the sequence of his sermon series and that on this occasion he might preach on prayer for the world (which was listed in their newsletter for two weeks' time), rather than the sick. Then, I'd reorder it something like this:

> Hymn
> Prayer of adoration
> 3 songs of worship
> Children's address
> Baptism
> Announcements
> Offering
> Sermon on prayer for the world
> Talk with missionaries
> Prayer for others and the world
> Song
> Benediction

In this order I have established the service with a solid worship and prayer time first. The children's address would be about telling children everywhere about Jesus, and would culminate in the baptism of the child with the children watching.[10] The announcements and offering provide a natural break, but then the sermon picks up on the theme of bringing Jesus to all nations through prayer. The talk with the missionaries would be a practical outpouring of the subject matter, and the intercessory prayer could then gather all that had happened in the service, with a focus on the gospel

---

[10] While we want to assist a family with a child, we should remember that a baptism is the conduct of a sacrament—one of only two in most denominations—and a high point of faith for the church as well as the person being baptized. As the church's 'initiation rite' it should not be downplayed or just placed for convenience.

reaching every land to make disciples for Jesus.

That is not the only possible solution! There are a number of others that would serve well too. But the important lesson here is to **start asking the right questions about creating a flow and a direction for the service content that takes people logically and easily from one part to the next.**

So when you schedule a song in your service, it's not just about writing its name on a song list. Make sure it fits in with what is happening around it. The visitor from Gideons will talk about handing out Bibles—how will that be blended into the service? What will you do just before it? How will you take people on to the next part of the service from there?

When you start to look for, and answer, those questions for every part of your service plan, you will start to realise whether the worship will "flow" and whether its "direction" at any given point is helpful to the overall theme, whether the segment you are dealing with is a song, hymn, prayer, missionary spot or barbecue announcement. Get the idea?

To help you get started in this, I will set out some service plans below, one each in traditional, modern and blended styles, and make comments on each to try and point out how the flow is seeking to be achieved. You will probably be more familiar with one style than the other two, but read them all—you will learn from each one.

I will use what I believe are well known songs and hymns, because I don't want you missing the point due to not knowing the music I refer to. That means they may not be the latest and greatest, but that's the best way I can think of to illustrate the techniques. Beware, these are very limited illustrations, because without scripting every word it's impossible to show the flow and direction completely. But I hope there will be some ideas shown that will start you off on the right track.

OUTLINE OF A TYPICAL <u>TRADITIONAL</u> SERVICE

Call to Worship
Hymn
Prayers of Adoration and Confession
Declaration of Forgiveness
Doxology
First Reading
Psalm
Second Reading
Gospel
Hymn
Sermon
Offering
Notices
Prayers of Intercession
Passing of the Peace
Hymn
Holy Communion:
      Creed
Narrative of the Lord's Supper
      Great Prayer of Thanksgiving
      The Lord's Prayer
      Breaking of the Bread (and raising of the Cup)
      Lamb of God
      Communion
      Prayer after Communion
Hymn
Blessing/Dismissal/Benediction[11]

This will look like a very prescriptive order of service to most modern eyes. It is drawn from a formal service order of the

---

[11] For example, see: *Uniting in Worship* (1988), Joint Board of Christian Education, Uniting Church Press, Melbourne, p58-68.

Uniting Church in Australia, though relatively few congregations would follow it in its entirety. It comes with many directions and suggestions for its use, including the insertion of choir anthems, the wearing of appropriate liturgical colours, the use of the Church's lectionary for readings and so on, all of which is marvellously helpful when preparing worship of this type.

Its writers advise that it is designed into four segments—the gathering, the Word, the Communion and the sending out. You can see those sections—the first from the Call to Worship down to the Doxology (an outburst of praise and thanksgiving, usually sung); the second from the first reading to the sermon; the third the indented part covering the Communion; and the final sending out. To me it also includes what I would call a segment of response to the Word, from the Offering to the hymn before Communion (although a hymn in that place in a service is often used to lead people into Communion and could easily be counted as part of Communion).

There is a sense of flow and direction generated by this order—what I would call a "logical flow". That is the starting point for any service. The more spiritual, sensual flow and direction only come when the order specifies particular hymns, readings, theme, sermon topic, the content of the prayers and the way in which the Communion is conducted. In other words, **this is a good skeleton** for a traditional service**, it will gain flesh when the specifics are decided,** and it will **gain life when God breathes into it all by his Spirit.** We can't do the last part—God does that "live" on the day.

But let's insert some specifics to "flesh" the order out, and make some comments about them.

Theme: **Christlike character**

Call to Worship

Hymn: **O for a thousand tongues to sing**

(AHB[12] 141, TIS[13] 210, tune Lyngham)

This is a great hymn of praise, with the first five verses referring to different characteristics of Jesus, and the last asking God for power to spread the Word. The tune Lyngham is a soaring masterpiece of joy that provides repetition of key phrases and a counterpoint melody giving men and women separate harmonies to blend together.

Greeting

Prayers of Adoration and Confession:

I'd suggest a free prayer of praise and adoration, focussing on God's character—mercy, compassion, wisdom, grace, faithfulness etc. This could be followed with a confessional prayer—either free or from a prayer book—but one that has us admit our shortcomings: the fact that we do not have the character of Christ.

Declaration of Forgiveness

Doxology

First Reading: **Galatians 5:22-26**

Psalm: 103:1-11

Second Reading: **Colossians 3:10-14**

Gospel: **Matthew 7:1-5**

Hymn: **I will sing the wondrous story**

(AHB 173, TIS 233 v1-4, tune Hyfrydol)

This hymn celebrates the "story" of the readings, and personalizes the relationship between Christ and the singer, focussing on Jesus' grace, forgiveness, love and guiding presence. The last verse is not necessary in our context as it journeys off to heaven—and our communion with the saints

---

[12] Australian Hymn Book.

[13] *Together in Song,* the revised Australian Hymn Book.

of old is covered by the content of the chorus anyway. The tune is inventive, joyful and melodic.

Sermon: **Christlike character**

This sermon starts from the Gospel reading, noting how easily we judge others. Throwing the spotlight back upon ourselves, the distinction is made between reputation (what others think you are like) and character (who you really are). Discussing Christ's character, the attributes of humility (Phil 2:5-8), courage (John 18:33-35), vision (Mark 10:33) and discipline (Mark 1:35) are highlighted, with a final discussion of love as Christ's "character integrator", which is the element that draws all the other facets together (Col 3:14). It ends by imploring us to become like Christ in the way we live our daily lives (Gal 5:22-26).

>Offering
>Notices
>Prayers of Intercession:

Taking up the theme, these prayers could include nation, business and community leaders, that they would exhibit Christlike character, while we too would play our part in building a noble and just society.

>Passing of the Peace
>Hymn: **When I survey the wondrous cross**
>(AHB 258, TIS 342, tune Rockingham)

This hymn is a deeply personal response to the cross—perfect as a reflection on the character of Christ and as a preparation for Communion.

>Holy Communion:
>>Creed
>Narrative of the Lord's Supper
>>Great Prayer of Thanksgiving
>>The Lord's Prayer
>>Breaking of the Bread (and raising of the Cup)
>>Lamb of God

Communion
Prayer after Communion
Hymn: **Almighty Father of all things that be**
(AHB 530 v 1,4,5,6. Tune Chilton Foliat)
This hymn asks God to take our life and work and accept it as our living sacrifice. It's perfect for the challenge of taking the character of Christ into our lives. Verses 2 and 3 focus on God's work in creation and are unhelpful to our theme. The tune is uplifting and it makes a positive package to end the service.

Blessing/Dismissal/Benediction

As with any service, what is said and done in the in-between bits will be crucial to the flow and direction achieved. I have not specified content of the Communion, as in many traditional services this is dictated by set liturgies, but where there is flexibility it would be possible for the priest/minister/pastor to anchor it to the service theme with references to the character of Christ during prayers and other input.

OUTLINE OF A TYPICAL <u>MODERN</u> SERVICE

Worship songs and prayers
Announcements
Offering
(Communion)
Sermon
Prayer time
Song
Dismissal

This order of service will look bare and even inadequate to those from a traditional background. I have constructed it from my observations of worship in churches like the Australian Christian Churches (formerly Assemblies of God) and the Vineyard.

There are essentially three parts to the service: a time of worship; a time of teaching; and a time of ministry. But it's not quite as simplistic as it may first appear.

The worship time includes a number of songs (and occasionally, a hymn), interspersed with prayer and Scripture readings as the worship leader feels is appropriate. Then there is a "break" for the announcements and the offering (sometimes an "offering sermon" is included here—a five to ten minute explanation of Christian giving and an encouragement to do so). If Communion is to be celebrated it usually follows here.

The second main section is the teaching time, comprising the sermon, in which the preacher usually references the Bible either by preaching through a passage or linking verses from various books to provide an overall view of his/her subject.

The third part of the service covers response to the Word, and often includes an altar call (an invitation to go to the front for prayer for healing or prayer on a subject of spiritual growth related to the message).

As a skeleton it doesn't tell us much about what to expect, so let's flesh it out and see what it presents.

> *Theme:* **Soft hearts, hard feet** (the practice of Christian love)

Worship songs and prayers:

> **Come, now is the time to worship** (P&W[14] 900)

---

[14] All references to P&W song numbers are from the Praise & Worship

This is a good standard opening song, inviting people into God's presence just as they are.[15]

Blessed be Your name (Redman) (P&W 994)

This song opens up the theme a little, by discussing good and hard times, whilst remaining a song that moves along.

10,000 reasons (Redman)

This song slows the pace a bit and deepens the worship, maintaining the idea of making worship a whole-of-life event.

Above all (P&W 940)

This song continues honouring God, but introduces the notion of sacrifice, and what Christ has done for us.

Thank You Lord (P&W 890)

This song takes this further, and involves people in deep worship and thanksgiving for what Christ has done. It's a great basis on which to pick up the theme of being people who practise the compassion and sacrifice of Christian love.

Musically, the songs start off upbeat and bright, deepening into slower and more profound worship. The keys the songs are played in are easily linked, providing smooth musical transitions.

> Announcements
> Offering
> Sermon: **Soft hearts, hard feet**

This is a sermon that focuses on the practice of Christian love in the world, under a title phrase made famous by Hong Kong evangelist Jackie Pullinger. It commences by underlining that love is a choice and an action, not just a fuzzy feeling, and the

---

Resource Song Books by Resource Christian Music, eg. *Praise & Worship Volume E* (2002), Resource Christian Music, Shannon Books & RCM Publications, for song numbers 858-928.

[15] You can sing this amazing song a bit slower later in a service and it becomes a deep invitation into true worship.

Bible stresses that we are to relate to each other in love. The bulk of the message is an exposition of 1 Corinthians 13, contrasting Compassion and Acceptance (soft hearts) with Sacrifice and Endurance (hard feet)—all being essential qualities of the love we are to express in the world. It concludes with a reference to soft hands and hard feet producing big smiles (Psalm 28:7), both for the loved and the loving.

Prayer time

Song: **The Potter's hand** (P&W 857)

This song implores Christ to use us for his kingdom, and underlines the message with a great statement of pious commitment.

Dismissal

As noted earlier, this style of service relies on the skill of the worship leader to offer appropriate prayer. Opportunity exists for prayers of adoration early in the worship bracket, and confession connected with the songs about the cross later in the bracket. The prayer time after the sermon would focus on personal growth and commitment.

OUTLINE OF A TYPICAL <u>BLENDED</u> SERVICE

Call to Worship
Hymn
Prayer
Welcome and Notices
Offering
Songs
Children's time/greeting   (Communion)
Testimony
Intercessory Prayer
Bible Reading

Sermon
Song or Hymn
Ministry Prayer
Benediction

This order is a real hybrid of the two earlier styles, and is one I inherited from one of the churches I served. It had grown out of an amalgamation of two former services, one traditional and one modern, and so has elements of both. It opens rather formally with a call to worship and a hymn, contains a bracket of newer songs focussing on worship a little further in. It treats the offering as part of the worship. The children's time is followed by a time of greeting as the children depart, and a testimony if available. The intercessory prayer comes before the Word. A song or hymn consolidates the teaching, and ministry prayer is offered as people leave.

As a service its logic flows well, though it needs patience from both traditionalists and contemporary worshippers to make it successful. Let's flesh it out now.

Theme: **Facing life's seasons with confidence**
Call to Worship
Hymn: **All things bright and beautiful** (AHB 70)
This hymn is bright and well known, and discusses God's hand in creation and the seasons. It provides a beginning to the subject.

Prayer
Welcome and Notices
Offering
Songs: **Faithful God** (P&W 633)
Faithful God is a gentle song, reminding us of the way God cares for us in all situations.

Made me glad (Hillsong[16] "Blessed")

Made me glad takes this notion deeper, with a very personal statement about God's care in difficult times.

How great is our God (Passion[17])

The move from there into a strong worship song, *How Great is our God* lifts the worship experience from the purely personal to a grand collective statement of God's timelessness and supremacy over all things.

> Children's time/greeting   (Communion)
> Testimony
> Intercessory Prayer
> Bible: **Ecclesiastes 3:1-11**
> Sermon: **Facing life's seasons with confidence**

This is a sermon centred on Ecclesiastes 3—a time for every purpose. Noting that life's seasons are often confusing, beyond our control and both good and bad, the message reassures people that God finds a purpose for each one (Rom 8:28). It challenges hearers to find what is most important in the season they are in, to learn from it, and to find ways of enjoying it and helping others in the midst of it.

> Ministry Prayer
> Song: **I will run to you** (P&W 802)

I will run to You completes the statements about God and his faithfulness in a song that invites the singer to trust God and the moving of his Spirit in every season of our lives.

> Benediction

I hope that by looking over these brief constructions you will understand why I have chosen certain hymns and songs and made other suggestions of content, and that you will have

---

[16] Hillsong Music is published by the Hillsong Church, Sydney.
[17] Passion 05, published by Worship Together, Brentwood TN, USA.

started to see the flow and direction induced by those choices. If you have, you're on your way!

IMAGINATIVE WORSHIP

Earlier we mentioned creativity as an opportunity for worship, and all of the services outlined above can be supplemented with, or even at times replaced by, other forms of imaginative worship. Our five senses all offer possibilities for lifting people beyond themselves and into the presence of God, and also enable us to thank God for the multiple ways he has given us to perceive his creation and understand his own nature.

I'm no expert on the arts, and there are plenty of others who have written helpful material to get you going with the specifics of using the arts in church. My point here really is to talk about the impact of creativity and its integration into worship and to promote its use. I'll suggest some broad possibilities as examples of what I'm talking about, and then your own creativity can take over from there.

Every church service has a setting, whether it's in a cathedral, a weatherboard chapel, a gymnasium or the great outdoors. When you prepare worship it is important to keep in mind where the events will happen. While as a modern churchgoer I have at times scoffed at some quite misplaced liturgical processions, the impact of such pageantry in a cathedral is awesome. Singing, and sound generally, is problematic outside unless you have access to good public address (sound) equipment. Many "old" churches need to pay attention to their setting if they are to house a service that is "modern".

The setting you are in can be modified to great effect with the use of lighting, backdrop, sound and even atmosphere. A shaft of light, the thunder of an organ, the aroma of incense, the mystery of a "smoke" machine, the disembodied voice speaking the Word, can all vary the setting of worship and stimulate the worshippers in new and exciting ways.

Static displays can be used to amplify a theme visually. A stark cross, a flickering candle, a beam of light through a prism, a statue, a banner or a dramatic picture can all excite the senses and draw a congregation into the subject matter of the service.

The possibilities for the use of the dramatic arts in worship are almost endless. When used in an appropriate setting they add impact to the worship—from plays and poetry to movies and clowns.

Unless a particular play almost becomes the entire service for a day, plays are best kept short and to the point. Use them to tell a story or make a single, profound point, and then elaborate on it in various ways through the rest of the service. When using a play as "the service" **make sure that it does actually provide people with worship, and not simply entertainment or theatre.** You need to think about how you are helping the congregation to connect with the drama and to personally and collectively offer their thoughts, feelings and spiritual leadings to God as worship. A well-chosen song or hymn, a carefully worded prayer or a guided time of silence might achieve what you need.

With the use of data projectors and sound equipment, the impact of a scene from a well-known movie can be telling. The current trend is to use clips from movies as part of the teaching time, where the context of the clip can be explained and the desired point can be immediately amplified. Using movie excerpts as thought-provokers or in other ways is possible too, but they can also distract your people into the rest of the movie and away from the service, unless your use of it is well-controlled.

One of the key reasons for using creativity in worship is, of course, to involve the congregation. And rather than simply stimulating them, it is often helpful to find ways of getting the people active rather than being passive observers of the service.

There are many ways to do that. Traditional ways have included hymn singing, responsive readings, and collective prayer (like the Lord's Prayer). Apart from music, which this book will deal with extensively later on, church people can participate in such activities as processions, altar calls, group prayer, discussion groups, quizzes, café church and dancing, to name a few I've seen recently. All of these require careful management in order to retain a sense of worship, but all are valid expressions of it.

Remember that you need to think about the **overall unity and direction** of the worship you are planning. In other words, don't plan creative elements that "clash" with each other. Keep the brass band out of the meditation time! Don't use incense in a café church. Don't try to floodlight a stark cross if the rest of the service is bright and lively. Use elements that promote a certain mood, befitting the subject you are dealing with. If something jars, save it for another service and cut it from this one. You'll do yourself and your people a big favour if you do.

The other temptation that arises when a creative team gets active is that everything gets sacrificed on the altar of the novel component. Remember that what you are doing is **applying a tool to help people worship God**. Don't let your creativity become an idol.

Many of these ideas are better for **occasional use**—it's rare that a church can mount creative worship like this every week and do it successfully. At some point your church will settle into a style of worship that is "normal" for them, given the particular mix of gifts and skills you have available. The point is to introduce creativity to add variety to that norm or to make a special impact for a short season. Think of creative ways to break out of the rut—whether it's a traditional or a modern one—by varying things enough each week to build an air of expectation about your services. It's a joy when people are coming to worship and wondering, "What might happen today?"

Creativity is a gift from God. Use it.

5 MUSIC FOR WORSHIP

...I love the ability to express through song the things I could never put into just the spoken word...[18]

We are now (finally, I hear you cry!) moving squarely into the more detailed and technical realm of the music.

Believe me, what has gone before was a necessary journey! If you think you are just there to sing or play, then think again. **Preparing and performing music in a worship context is quite different from a normal "gig"**. All that has gone before in this book provides the background, the purpose and the context for the worship music that you are planning and playing.

Without knowing those things you would be operating in the dark and worship would suffer accordingly, becoming inconsistent in quality and style, and uneven in purpose and meaning. So if you've picked up this pocketbook for a few ideas on the music side, and haven't read the rest, do yourself a favour and schedule some time to read the first four sections—you will emerge better prepared if you do.

We have already begun to discuss music in the context of its contribution to flow and direction in a service. As we discuss

---

[18] Darlene Zschech: "The True Value of Worship", (2010) YouTube video (https://www.youtube.com/watch?v=FvwQMvopyNU).

the music itself we will, by necessity, go over that ground some more, but I hope that a little repetition will reinforce the ideas about both as we get deeper into it.

Remember that earlier we stressed the power of music to engage people and to teach them. We also called it the primary participatory element of corporate worship. So let's start our discussion of music where we left off—at how it contributes to worship.

PLANNING THE MUSIC CONTENT OF A SERVICE

Music will make contributions right through the service, in those four major areas of entering, worshipping, learning and responding that we discussed, and in other more subtle ways as well.

Beginning a service can happen with a mighty song or hymn of praise, or with a gentle, inviting song that helps people enter into the service. Both are valid. A common pattern is for a song (or songs) or hymn of praise (or both) which allows the hubbub of the time of entering to refocus into the expression of love for God. It's harder (but not impossible, and very effective) to start more quietly and "build up" the sound and energy of the music further into the service.

Many elements contribute to worship. As we have discussed, actions such as prayer, testimony, and our offerings add to the communal worship experience. **But music is vital. It is the primary means of corporate worship; it is the vehicle that opens doors to hearts.** You can create a progression in worship through song—for example, from fast and exuberant praise, through quiet confessional songs and on into grand songs of uplifting worship; or from quiet, reflective songs, building up to joyous praise.

Often songs need to lead people into special moments like

communion, so choose songs that create the right atmosphere and mood for people to engage with those moments. And of course, many churches use incidental music to support the prayers, to good effect.

Music can contribute to the preaching of the Word. If you're choosing songs or hymns for around the time of the Bible reading or sermon, select a song or songs that will help to open up and amplify the theme of the day.

Alongside prayer, offerings, faith statements, "going forward" and so on, **songs help people respond to God's word**, and to go into the world renewed. A song that picks up the message of the sermon—and helps people express that idea through singing—can help people take it home in their hearts. Many modern songs are helpful for this—they express piety (our devotion to God), and very often in a personal way ("I" songs: we'll discuss this further on).

HYMNS

We mentioned earlier how the music of the church gets sifted by time. So, for example, very few hymns are still sung that date from the time of the Reformation or before. One or two of Luther's hymns are around (unless you're a Lutheran and still use lots!). Most hymns used in churches now date from the 18th and 19th Centuries, and from particular outpourings of the Spirit, like the time of John and Charles Wesley.

Some hymns are classics, and will live on for centuries yet. In a sense, we should ensure they are not forgotten: they are a crucial part of the church's heritage. But it's also true that some have faded with time, and their use only tends to perpetuate a bygone era. Which category a particular hymn fits in will vary from person to person and congregation to congregation. A hymn that is of vital importance to one church may hold no meaning for another down the road.

Hymns frequently take a topic and develop it verse by verse. Sometimes this is helpful and sometimes not. It's wonderful if your service is on a theme and your hymn picks up on it from several viewpoints. But it can be frustrating, for example, if every hymn you sing ends up joyously around God's throne in heaven when the point you were trying to make was about life here and now. Sometimes you may want to select particular verses to include or leave out.

Within their own genre, hymns cover the same range of styles that more modern songs do. Some are praise, some are worship, some are about our commitment to faith. Some are faster, or louder, some are softer, more worshipful or reflective. Use them accordingly!

Hymns follow a strong pattern in construction. They are poetic, usually having strong rhyme and rhythm. In fact, each one will have a designated number of syllables in each line of the verse. This is called the metre. Hymn tunes can often be swapped around because of this. If you like the words of a particular hymn but the set tune is unfamiliar or unsuitable to your purpose, then it is often possible to find another tune in the hymn book that the words will fit.

Above each hymn, near the title, you will usually find the metre recorded. The name of the tune, say HYFRYDOL, will be there, and then some numbers—in this case 87.87 D—appears. That means that the hymn tune allows for eight syllables in the first line, seven in the second, eight in the third and seven in the fourth. The "D" means "double"—a repeat of that same pattern. So the tune supports an eight-line stanza, with the first line of 8 syllables, then 7 in the second, then, 8, then 7, 8, 7, 8 and finally 7 syllables. Occasionally, a hymn will be listed with no numbers—just the letters "C.M." Those letters simply mean "common metre"—so any hymn with C.M. can be swapped in the same way.

So if you came across a hymn whose tune is not familiar, but that has really good words for your purpose, you can look at the metre of the tune, and often find another tune with that same metre and use that. It's a really handy trick, but it does have an occasional pitfall, like if the tune requires the singer to hold a note, but that note falls in the middle of a word and makes it sound strange. In other words, always check that the tune will work by **singing every verse through beforehand to make sure** there are no quirks that will distract the congregation.

Also churches do become accustomed to singing hymns to particular tunes, so you might lose a few friends if you alter their favourites. And be aware that **the new tune you select will give the hymn a different "flow"**. It might now be brighter—or duller—than you intended and that new flow needs to be taken into account in your service plan.

Modern hymns, like their more contemporary song counterparts, vary dramatically in quality—they haven't yet been through the sifting of time. Some, like Stuart Townend's "In Christ Alone" soar with the best—but many others don't. A significant number of the modern hymns I've heard suffer from the same flaw as many modern songs—they have us at the centre with God portrayed more as our benevolent helper than the focus of our worship.

Seek out hymns that stay close to the gospel. Hymns that focus more on, say, environmental messages like caring for the planet, or are trying to be relevant by using references to TV sets and police cars, are often corny to sing, and can seem more like promotion of a particular viewpoint under a pretence of worship. As Paul said,

> *...I did not come with eloquence or human wisdom as I proclaimed to you the testimony about God. For I resolved to know nothing... except Jesus Christ and him crucified. (1 Corinthians 2:1-2)*

The closer the words stay to the great messages of the Scriptures, the safer they are (that's true of modern songs as well!).

SONGS

There has been a tsunami of new songs for worship swamping the world in recent years. From a trickle in the 1960s to a flood in the 80s and a complete deluge today, songs can be sourced from anywhere, and most churches of any size will have an individual or even a team writing songs for them. That's how Hillsong became world renowned, with worship pastors whose job descriptions included song writing (of course, they were very good at it!).

That means that every church has an amazing choice, and the **repertoires of congregations vary enormously**. There are some songs that become popular and we all end up singing them at some point, but overall there is a diversity that has grown in the last 20 years and every church you visit is singing a different list of songs. Some of them are home-grown and encourage your people because they know the writer, but often it's just because different songs appeal to different people and there are so many to choose from.

Some songs are classics and will work well in many situations and for many years. Some have a shorter lifespan, and that's OK. If there's a pattern, I think that churches tend to be less discriminating in what they introduce and then find that the song wasn't as good as they first thought and it drops off the play-list.

I try to look for songs that will have a longer life cycle and are more reliable theologically. Remember earlier when we discussed the power of music? It's very easy to inadvertently teach bad theology through poorly written songs that get stuck in people's minds. Current songs haven't had the years of sifting that older music has had, so we have to be discerning and do some of that work ourselves. **Every song should be considered carefully for what it says before you use it.** Some writers, looking to "find a new angle" will introduce a new name for God, or a trendy catchphrase that works rhythmically, in the hope of producing something new and potentially popular. My alarm bells ring when I see these techniques. **This kind of manipulation in the lyrics often points to shaky theology and ultimately, a song that isn't worth the trouble of learning**.

Songs cover the whole raft of worship music, from praise and worship, through piety and commitment, thanksgiving and testimony. Occasionally you will find a song written from God's perspective. These require careful handling and are often best done as a solo.

Many writers seem to be seeking the "ultimate" intimate worship song, and get very personal in their language. But there's a danger with that if the song is not written carefully: some quite popular songs are sung to "you" and don't name Jesus or God or any of the key facts of the gospel, and could be addressed to almost anyone from Allah and Buddha to the girl next door!

In the same vein, **many popular worship songs use the word "I"**. While we want to have songs that speak deeply of our relationship to God in worship, many of the current songs being used as worship I would classify more tightly as songs of piety (expressing personal devotion to God) rather than true worship (honouring God for who he is).

The phrase "I worship you" can have as its focus either the "I" or the "you". When considering these songs, look closely at the whole of the song's lyrics and work out where the balance lies. A song that says "I worship you, I give my life for you, I will follow you all my days" is talking primarily about the singer, not the one being worshipped. A song that says, "I worship you, for you are holy, you are righteous, I bow my knee before your throne" has God as its primary focus and is more worshipful than the other example which is one of piety.

There are **two problems** that arise if "I" songs are over-used. The first is that **congregational singing is also about us worshipping together** (this was one of our goals for corporate worship), so songs that link us are helpful too: "we" and "our" and "us" do this, especially early in the service when we want to express that unity of purpose as we come together.

The second problem with "I" songs is that **some of them are much more about "I" than about God.** Don't spend a whole service telling God how good "I" am for worshipping him—tell him how good he is for loving and saving us!

The content of the words of the songs in a recent service I attended could be summed up as saying, "I've come here for you, now please God come here and show me your love and power and presence so that I can feel good". OK, I'm exaggerating a little but you get the point. Unusually for this church, where the worship is often excellent, there was no song that mentioned the cross, and only one out of five that named Jesus. The rest of the songs chosen that day only named "you"—when they weren't talking about "I". I was worried inside about whether the worshippers had been led to focus on God or themselves. As we have said, music is powerful and it's easy to learn the wrong things through it, and days like that one can start a slippery slope to self-interest.

In a stark contrast I went to that same church to hear a visiting songwriter and worship leader lead the same band and the same people right to the throne-room of the Father. There were six songs; only one mentioned "I" and all of them focussed on God and his holiness, grace, mercy, faithfulness, love and the power of the cross. The Spirit of God hovered amazingly in that room and when the music faded we stood spellbound for over five minutes of silence, soaking in the presence of the Lord. That's the difference.

One or two songs of piety will probably be important to your theme and direction on any given Sunday, but be careful to put them into the ultimate context—that we love and follow Jesus Christ because of who he is and what he has done for us.

Let me offer two examples. Joel Houston's "Everyday"[19] and Brooke Fraser's "Desert Song"[20] are both strong songs of piety. They offer lyrics of deep commitment and faith, and encourage the singer to live out the Christian life in good times and bad. But don't offer them to God *on their own* as a substitute for true worship (honouring God for who he is): they are about us, not him.

From what we have said earlier on service design, it's clear that pious songs belong best as a statement of our response to God and his Word. So as a guide I suggest that **after the sermon—when we are thinking about how to respond to God's love—is usually the most appropriate place for them**. Just as "we" songs unite us in worship at the start, so "I" songs help us to go out as individuals to face our world. When you place them elsewhere (as I have often done—there are so many of them!) be sure why you are doing so and the context in which it happens (in other words, be aware of your direction and flow—see those sections above).

---

[19] Joel Houston, "Everyday", © 1999 Hillsong Publishing, Castle Hill, NSW.
[20] Brooke Fraser (Ligertwood), "Desert Song", © 2008 Sony/ATV Music Publishing Australia.

MUSIC SELECTION

Let's now talk about the business of song selection more directly in the context of all that we have already learned about planning worship. The way you select your songs will have a powerful effect on how your service works. It is, in fact, the single most significant effect after the theme and sermon, and sometimes even ahead of those: the power of music.

There are several aspects to keep in mind as you choose the music content of the service, most of which we've touched on in other discussions. Let's list them systematically here.

Think about the **purpose** of the singing at that point in the service. Praise, worship, reflection, confession, storytelling, prayer, statements of belief and declarations of commitment are all able to be explored in song. Or your purpose might be the dedication of an offering, or the introduction to Communion. In a service you will probably be including a number of these, but be sure about which purpose is foremost when considering a particular song. Don't forget also that enjoyment is a legitimate sub-plot—especially with children and youth.

Consider the **words** you will be singing. Look for phrases that are important to the song's message, or phrases or choruses that are repeated often—they usually tell you a lot about what the song is saying. Do these suit the service theme? Does this song fit better before or after another that you're considering? This song has one really good line, but does the rest of it help or hinder? Does it fit the theme of the service? Does it fit what is planned around it, or will it jar?

Consider the **direction** in which each song is leading people's thoughts. You will want to ensure that, when combined, they produce a "journey" which starts at one point and takes people to another, and that the result is a mood appropriate to the end purpose of the singing.

Consider the **style** of each song you are choosing. Which part of the service does the song best fit? Is it praise, thanksgiving, piety or worship? Is it upbeat or more reverent? Is it a song to sing near the start of a service, or when you're preparing to leave—a song of commitment? Will it create a mood of joy or thoughtfulness or challenge or humility?

Consider the **tempo** (speed) of the song. A fast song after a couple of slow ones will break the mood you have set. That may be a good thing, or it may not, depending upon what you are seeking to achieve.

Consider the **flow** of worship. Flow is affected not just by the words but also by "mechanical" things like the tempo and the key that it is in, and the mood that the song creates.

Consider the **direction of the whole worship experience**. Are the songs you have linked together taking the service as a whole in a helpful direction? Is that direction consistent with the theme of the service? If you can't answer a resounding "yes" to those questions for each song, ask yourself again why you chose it (them) and look for alternatives.

Let me offer **a practical example** at this point about how you might consider the choice of a song. Take the song, "The Power of Your Love" by Geoff Bullock.[21] This song, written in the late 1980s, swept around the world in contemporary worship settings and found its way into more traditional worship as well (TIS 685). It is still often used, as it should be—it's a great song!

So let's think about the contribution it might make to your service. It's a song that explores the singer's relationship with God, and expresses a longing to be close to God and empowered by his love. Its tempo is moderate, so it doesn't

---

[21] Geoff Bullock "The Power of Your Love", © 1992 Nightlight Music (Aust). P&W 621.

lend itself instantly as an opening song. It belongs more to themes of commitment and worship than praise or thanksgiving. Its very personal references are full of a pious desire to be nearer to God.

Now let's think about its placement in your service. It starts like this:

> *Lord I come to You*
> *let my heart be changed, renewed*

Because of that opening, many churches use it in the early part of a service. From those words it sounds like it's a song that brings you in from outside—and it can if used well. But when you think about those words in the context of the whole song, they are revealed as words of response, saying something like, "now that I've heard anew today of your love, I want to come to you and be renewed in it". So its logical place is after the sermon as a response. In fact, having considered the whole song you might agree with me that it is much more of a response song than a beginning one.

I am NOT saying that you can only use it at the end of a service! I think it is best placed there most of the time, as it is primarily a song of commitment. But **you can facilitate its use in other ways by what is said and done around it.** If the point of your opening of worship is to identify with people's hunger for God and to get them to open up to his love, then the song can be powerful in that context. But that context needs to be established—by what is said or done preceding the song—in order for it to work best for you.

So when you schedule the "The Power of Your Love" in your service, it's not just about writing its name on a song list. What is being said, prayed or done around it that establishes accurately how you are using the song? The song ends with a chorus that focuses strongly on living our lives in the power of God's love. What will you do straight after it? How will you take people on to the next part of the service from there?

Another example may help in terms of finding the best song rather than just a good one. I attended a service recently whose theme was about us serving others and not sitting back expecting to be served. The reading was from Mark 10 about James and John requesting to be seated at Jesus' right and left hands in his Kingdom, which culminates in Christ saying that he had come to serve and give his life as a ransom for many (10:35-45).

The song chosen to end the service was Graham Kendrick's classic song, "The Servant King".[22] Its first three verses discuss the sacrifice Christ made in coming to earth and dying for our sins, and the last verse talks about us learning to serve as Christ had modelled. It was a strong choice. For that service I would have chosen it too.

But was it the best song to go out on? It is a strong song but not a commanding one. Finishing the service with it was "satisfying" but not "challenging"; it "completed" the service but did not "punctuate" it.

My suggestion is this (and remembering there are many solutions to these things): use that song between the Bible reading and the sermon as a strong foretaste of the message and finish instead with Darlene Zschech's monumental "The Potter's Hand".[23] The chorus of that song—*take me, mould me, use me, fill me, I give my life to the Potter's hand*—I think would have provided the power and challenge to end the service with a real message in song for the congregation to have in their heads as they went into the world. It's not that the Kendrick song was wrong—it was good—but to my mind

---

[22] Graham Kendrick, "From heaven you came", © 1983 Thankyou Music, P&W 674.
[23] Darlene Zschech, "The Potter's Hand", © 1997 Hillsong Australia, P&W 857.

there was a better way of using that one and finishing more powerfully with the other one (which wasn't chosen for the service).

Once you become more used to posing these sorts of questions and making decisions, you will find that ideas come more easily, bringing greater direction and flow to the services you plan. You will also find that when things are not right it will become more apparent; you will be more attuned to spotting likely problems and working through to find the right solution for that day.

Finding the right solution—that's the challenge. It's often a really tough decision as to whether to go with one song over another. Sometimes you will prefer a particular song because of the way the music works with songs around it. But when it comes down to **the bottom line, I choose the song that has the words that are right** for the day. Those words will keep your theme on track and amplify the message for the day. And if you have found a song whose words really "nail it" then work the other, less crucial songs around it so that its full power is brought out.

SONGS THAT FLOW

Creating flow and direction in a time of singing is a key to drawing people into the heart of worship. This is often enhanced when appropriate links between songs are constructed.

Songs flow into one another most easily when they are in the same key, have the same time signature, tempo and cover similar subject matter. But worship would end up pretty boring if the songs stayed so closely linked for the whole service, so it's helpful if at times we can build links that will sustain the flow of the worship but allow some broader options as we move from one song to another.

That can happen in a number of ways, and it's mostly the job of the musicians and the worship leader so I'll cover those more technical bits in the music and worship leading sections. The key point to do with selecting songs is to **have enough of an idea about how songs can be linked to know that your choices will work**.

Having given first consideration to the theme of the service and where you want to go with the words and the sound of the songs, look at how they might link musically by checking the key. The same key, or a tone higher (for example, C to D) is usually easy, as are the fourth and fifth chords of that key (in the key of C, they are F and G).

Note that it's almost always **better to move up a tone than down**. Going up lifts the worship onto that new level; going down tends to be a bit of a downer for the people. Try it and you'll soon see what I mean.

Equally importantly, **check the tempo**. If you have started with praise and you're trying to move toward worship, you'll want the tempo to slow. If you've just had a slow song, a faster one will probably break the mood for worship. If it is being chosen as an "in-between" song, then look for a tempo that is "in-between" as well. Other factors like the time signature (4/4, 3/4 etc.) are less critical but can have an effect.

If you do feel it's important to have the songs you've chosen but you're worried about the flow, then discuss the problem with your musicians and worship leader. There are tricks that they have that can make it all work (which we will discuss shortly) but the easier you can make it by choosing the best songs, the better.

MUSIC SELECTION RESOURCES

Choosing the right songs can seem an onerous task. When

you first start to do it you wonder where to even find a song list you can choose from! But there are ways to make your task easier.

The first is simply a matter of good record-keeping within your congregation, which I urge you to do. If you don't already maintain a record of the hymns and songs you have used, start one now. **A simple spreadsheet can keep track of the songs you have used**, where they are sourced (book, online etc), what key they are in, what theme they promote, what style, mood, tempo, and any other data you wish to collect. (Alternatively, software specifically created for this purpose can be used, if the budget allows—for example, Planning Center Services). My spreadsheet also made note of when we first used the song (often necessary for copyright reasons), how many times we had used it and what the dates of the most recent three uses were.

Apart from telling you instantly which songs your church knows and uses to aid song selection, this kind of information can quickly tell you helpful things like if you are over-using a song, which happens more than you would think! It's also a check on how recently you have used them, and you can also tell which songs you have used together (in the same service). In short, it's a primary resource for your song and hymn selection that you can create for yourself.

Another helpful way to progress your search for the right songs is to utilise the books you have. Most worship **song books and hymnals include their own indexes**, and most of them are more than just an alphabetical list. Often they include key, subject and Scripture references which can guide you to the right music for your service. Most hymn books also group the hymns in categories like hymns about the Trinity, hymns about Jesus, hymns for Communion, hymns about Christian living and so on. Pay attention to those sections— they will help you place the right hymn in the right part of a service.

Then, there are any number of **online resources** that host worship songs and can give you words, music, samples of what the song sounds like and so on.

The CCLI website,[24] which most churches use for their copyright obligations, is one classic example, with their SongSelect site that will record your usage of songs as you download them. A few minutes on the site each week will keep your church's copyright in order and provide access to an amazing list of worship material (available in formats for vocals, piano, guitar, brass, bass and drums) which is instantly transposable to the key you need.

---

[24] Christian Copyright Licensing International (See songselect.ccli.com)

6 PRESENTING THE MUSIC

Somehow, about forty percent of churchgoers seem to have picked up the idea that "singing in church is for singers". The truth is that "singing is for believers". The relevant question is not, "Do you have a voice?" but "Do you have a song?"[25]

Our role in leading worship is to invite and encourage all attendees to join in. But there seems to be a group of worshippers who struggle to participate, and to me that group seems to have grown a lot lately. **We need to try and help those people find their song.**

I've been to many churches of a number of different denominations, especially over the last three years since I was forced to retire with ill-health, and often I have come away disappointed by the worship. Sometimes the services suffered from poorly chosen and organised music (not flowing or directional), but a considerable part of it was about presentation. Too many churches are playing great songs that should produce worship and yet are somehow not inspiring their people to participate or to connect with God.

And it's not because the musicians were poor as musicians.

---

[25] Donald Hustad, as quoted in: E. K Rowell Ed. *Quotes for preaching and teaching from Leadership Journal*, 1996, Baker Books, Ada, Michigan, p184.

From my observation it was about presentation, and usually for one or more of a number of reasons:

- The **worship team were not a team**—they looked and sounded disinterested; or
- The **music team were more concerned about their own sound** than engaging with the congregation and drawing them in; or
- There was **little encouragement** from the worship leader for the people to participate; or
- The worship team were **too loud**.

OK, before you complain about that last one, let me explain. I'm not just saying that to protect my ageing ears: there is an important point here about worship. If you are in the midst of a congregation and the music is so loud that you cannot hear yourself sing, then whether you sing or not makes no difference. And when many ordinary, "non-musical" worshippers realise this they give up the struggle and just stop. And as I looked around many, many congregations, that's exactly what I saw—people just standing there, or chatting, or even texting on their mobile phones. They were totally disengaged from the worship, because they felt they couldn't make any difference by joining in.

If you think back to our original definitions of worship, then this constitutes a failure. **The point of gathering for worship is for us all to do it together**. If the people who are there to lead the congregation into the presence of God take over by volume or self-interest and make the people's contribution irrelevant, then they have defeated their own purpose. All the good work of preparing themed and flowing worship will come to nothing if it is not presented in a way that allows the people to connect with it and participate in it.

Traditional services have their issues too. There are **frequently services where there is no musical lead at all** and the congregation is left floundering with an unfamiliar hymn supported by an organist who doesn't emphasise the melody. The people stand bewildered, mouthing the words from the page but with no idea of how to produce worship out of their misery. This, too, is a failure in terms of what was intended when the worship was planned.

So I'm writing the sections on presenting music and leading worship in a desire to lift the quality of service leadership. **The band, the leaders of worship, need to both model worship and encourage worship**. I hope that as we work through the practical side of presenting worship you will discover the tools you need to help people engage with worship and unite with you in honouring God. That's the point of all that is to follow.

Those of you from traditional churches will quickly recognise that I am writing mostly about more contemporary worship, but don't despair. The primary role of the church choir, anthems notwithstanding, is to lead the people in their worship of God, and much of what follows will assist choirs to do that. And if you have no choir, think about the possibilities of a worship leader who can help the congregation into its music by providing a vocal lead and suitable encouragement.

The first thing to emphasise is to **do whatever you do to the absolute best of your ability**. If you are a gifted musician it's sometimes easy to just "wing it" and not put in much effort toward practice or performance. You may get away with that approach musically, but you will never feel truly satisfied that you have used your God-given gifts properly if you do that. You will have let yourself—and Jesus—down.

And if you are like me—an amateur musician trying to keep up with people who really know what they're doing—then put in the effort and make it as good as you possibly can. Learn all you can from the gifted people and apply it.

Part of doing your best is to **present yourself well**. I'm not suggesting for a moment that you should spend big money on clothes, hairdo and makeup. This is about presenting yourself well—sensibly and within your means. Guys, this means not just washing, but maybe even ironing your shirt!

Some churches establish **a dress code** for those at the front and I think that is helpful. But whether there is a code or not, remember that you are before God and his people leading worship of the Almighty One. It is not some gig somewhere, it is worship, and our desire is to honour God. So honour him by taking some care about your appearance.

Presenting yourself well includes **facial expressions**. A few weeks ago in a local church I experienced a first—I saw a bass player smile! People, if you are up front leading a congregation in a joyous expression of faith, then it should show! I'm not suggesting you grin like a Cheshire Cat. But let your own pleasure in worship show on your face and in your movement.

The other key point is to pray. **Commit everything you do personally to prayer, and pray with the team** you are working with. Pray for every aspect of your input, for the congregation and for the preacher, and invite the Holy Spirit to come, fill the place and amplify the worship.

SONG-LEADING: THE VOCALISTS

I know I keep saying it, but this is a different kind of performance. As a singer, you are providing the lead for the congregation, and enhancing the overall sound of the song with your ability to sing well and to harmonise. Your job is not to astonish everyone with your vocal cleverness, it is to make the worship sound better, so that God's people feel good about what is being presented to the Lord and lift their own efforts in support of it. With those objectives in mind, let's list some key factors to also keep in mind.

It seems like stating the obvious, but the first thing is to **know the songs**! You can't hope to lead a song that you don't know yourself, and if you are hesitant, the people will quickly discern it and copy it. They won't commit strongly to the melody or words if they are unsure about where they are going, and it's your job to take them there confidently.

Use your vocal power to **lead with your voice**. Don't expect the microphone to do all the work. It will only amplify what is there to be amplified. If your voice sounds weak and thin, then that weak and thin sound is what is amplified, so give a strong vocal output, without straining your vocal cords.

Learn how to use your microphone. Most vocal mics are unidirectional—that is, you need to sing directly into them, as opposed to an omnidirectional mic, which might be used to pick up a group of voices gathered around it. Sing into it as if it was an ice cream you were about to lick. Hold it about 2-3 cm from your lips and pointing directly at your mouth. And keep it there. The sound engineer cannot hope to keep your voice balanced with other musicians if you move it around all the time. There is a case for backing it away a few centimetres for a very loud or high note, but otherwise, consistency about where you hold the mic will give the best results.

Sing to the back. This does two things: it helps you use your vocal power well, and it helps to include everyone. If your eyes and vocal energy are directed at the first two rows, then those further back feel like they're missing out. If your gaze and your voice take in the whole room, then everyone can feel part of the worship. That's not to say that you can't look around—of course you can. But keep your "default" look toward the back.

Remember that **the first note and word are important**. The congregation will be looking to you to know when to come in. They will learn the song by what you do, so get it right and make the words clear and the entries sharp.

Relax and enjoy the music yourself. If someone on the team makes an error, don't turn and pull faces at them! If you are uptight the congregation will sense it. **Mistakes happen: get over it,** smooth out the problem in the easiest way possible, and make it seem like that's the way you meant it to be!

Remember that your **body language is important: you are modelling worship**. People will struggle to praise with you if everyone they see at the front is uptight, or angry at the others, or serious, or bored, or tired. Equally, false expressions and movements are at best, distracting and at worst, off-putting. Make sure that you are ready to fulfil your part. That means that you have had enough sleep, you are engaged with the music and your face and whole body moves appropriately with it. Put simply, the right body language will come from the right preparation—spiritually, emotionally and physically—and from the right attitude.

When **teaching a new song**, be sure to know it yourself, and sing in unison until you are sure that people have caught on to the melody.

Tempo is crucial. The right tempo produces the right mood for a song. Note that often large groups cannot keep up with a really fast tempo. However, be aware also that they sometimes drag a song unnecessarily. We'll say more on tempo shortly.

Keep alert and **watch both your other team members and the congregation for cues and pointers** that things are wrong. You can pick up feedback from the people and adjust what's happening as you go.

PLAYING IN GROUPS

Fortunately, the days of paid organists being the only music providers in the church have almost completely vanished, and most churches these days are blessed with at least a small team who present the music. Teamwork among these people will enhance the worship immeasurably.

The first thing to do is to **develop a team who see their music as a ministry**. As I have already said, playing music for worship is very different and I would rather have a less gifted musician who is deeply committed to the worship of Jesus, than a talented person who doesn't express love for the Lord in what they do. It's not just about being clever—worship is primarily about the heart and soul.

Developing your team will involve both **practice and prayer**. Musically you want to fine tune your interaction and your arrangements, and spiritually you want to find a unity of purpose and focus that brings you all to the same point on a Sunday. So practise and pray together.

Larger churches often have a number of musicians and singers who get rostered for various Sundays. This makes teamwork harder as it always seems that an individual is working with a different group of people each time they are rostered, and the outcome is often a group of people standing separately around a stage looking bored and doing their own thing.

To counter this in one church I was part of, we developed three distinct music teams, so those teams of people always worked together. The result was excellent: the teams became familiar with each other and developed their presentation, and it added variety to the music in our church as each band had a different mix of instruments and a unique sound. My group ended up as a band (with a name!) that played for many different inter-church events.

Practising on a weeknight is better than just before church. If you can do both, go for it! The separate midweek practice allows a relaxed time together. It's a chance to go over new material and get it right and an opportunity to think through all the musical linkages for Sunday. For example, the bridges between songs, music for prayer and offering, plans for Holy Communion and so on. It also offers the time needed to bond together and pray as a group.

Practice immediately **prior to the service** should really be a quick "freshen up" of what has already been planned. If you need to make that time your primary rehearsal, then be sure to allow sufficient time to work on all the necessary material—especially development of new songs.

Tune! It seems unnecessary to say it, except that I'm sure we have all cringed at some time because of a musician who didn't get it right. When I was a kid I was one of them! But these days tuning is able to be so much more precise. When I was young a guitar tuner would have cost me half a year's pocket money. Now tuners are both cheap and accurate. You can even get tuner apps for smartphones these days, so there is barely an excuse left for out of tune instruments—and it makes a huge difference when they are correct. And I don't just mean guitars—flutes, trumpets and any number of other instruments should be checked and tuned carefully before the start of a service.

Work as a team to **set the correct tempo for each song**. Usually the drummer does this, often from a metronome in their headphones set to the correct tempo found on the music chart.

Tempo has a powerful effect on any given song. Speaking very generally, praise is usually up-tempo (faster) and worship slower. I think, in part, that is due to the very nature of the two. Worship wants the time to know and explore every word; it wants to reach out into the deep places; it seeks the profound. Those things are more difficult to achieve in a faster praise song, whose goal is more likely to be celebration and joy. **Fast songs bring out joy and melody; slower ones bring out meaning and power. Sing a fast song too slow and you lose the joy. Sing a slow song too fast and you lose the power.**

A recent example of this for me was the slow, grand and powerful Matt Redman song, "10,000 Reasons". I sang it in the midst of the large congregation of a conference and not surprisingly, it lifted the room heavenward. There were smiles and tears. Some stretched their arms upward; some were on bended knee. The power of the song was enormous; electric.

Just a few days later, I was in the congregation of a small church whose band was just learning it, and they played it at what seemed close to double speed. It flopped to the point where I had to double check that I was singing the same song. I wouldn't have thought it possible, but it had lost all its grandeur and power, and there was no time to feast on the meaning of its wonderful phrases because the congregation was too busy trying to read the words on the wall fast enough to keep up. Worst of all, it completely lost that incredible "pregnant pause" just before you sing the last line of each verse, so the power of the "10,000s" was just absent.

I think of it this way. Matt Redman is a good musician. If the song was supposed to be played that fast, he would surely have done it. He doesn't. It's supposed to be slow. That's where so much of its impact comes from and Matt knows it.

In summary, **getting the tempo correct will boost your chances of creating meaningful worship—and getting it wrong can seriously damage them**.

Once the tempo is set, work as a group to keep it together. Listen for the drum beat and the bass notes to keep time, and adjust your playing and singing to blend in. Often groups speed up when they reach a familiar part like a chorus, so be alert for it and hold together.

Always work on **entrances and endings**. These make the music "tight" and give a better lead for the congregation.

Work on varying the **volume and power** of the songs in logical and helpful ways too. Often verses can be sung softer, with full power reserved for the chorus. Some songs require more vocal and instrumental energy than others.

But now we're starting to talk about arrangements, so let's do it properly.

ARRANGEMENTS

As soon as you start to sing or play a song, you are "arranging" it for your own voice or instrument. When you have a number of instruments and voices available it invites the possibility of arranging the music to add variety and produce musical highlights that enhance the worship.

Vocal arrangements vary from solos, duets and simple harmony right through to full choral work, barbershop quartets and jazz. Use the gifts you have. Vary from melody-only through to serious part-singing, with some verses or choruses softer, louder or more harmonised according to the emphasis the song requires. Some songs allow for parts for men and women in the way they are written, for example when the women "echo" a line.

Try to find ways of blending the voices you have together—it's not always easy. I found one solution when I was working with a woman who had quite a shrill, operatic soprano voice combined with rather poor diction, a combination that just sounded odd for modern church music. Challengingly for her, I had her sing nearer the bottom of her range and had a light baritone male sing a part higher than hers. This helped her voice blend in more and stopped that rather awkward effect of her voice sounding shrill and indistinct, and high above all the others.

Instrumental arrangements can be great fun too, and add a lot to the music. You can start simply with a guitar or piano, and build your arrangement adding bass, drums, electric lead guitar and highlight instruments like flute and trumpet. Maybe you're lucky enough to boast a whole brass section, or strings like violin and cello.

Work out arrangements that all players can participate in— **some keys are not easy for certain instruments**: for example, E Flat, B Flat and F are common keys for keyboard instruments but are more difficult for acoustic guitars, while brass instruments usually need transposed music.

"Bright" instruments like **brass and electric guitar** work well with **faster praise songs**, while **slower worship songs** often lend themselves to more **mellow sounds like cello and flute**. Of course, worship can build up into very grand music that includes everything!

The possibilities for variation are almost endless: you can change the instrument mix for different verses; you can change key; change tempo; add harmonies and backing vocals; do a line or verse unaccompanied; add an instrumental while a prayer is offered; or even insert all or part of another song and then return to the original song.

Here's **an example arrangement**, using the wonderful Melody Green song, "There is a Redeemer":[26]

Intro on acoustic guitar, finger-picking style, with first verse solo by a competent female vocalist; repeat the first verse for congregational singing bringing in piano and violin; add bass and drums for the first chorus; second verse add a vocal harmony, and also flute, and lead guitar for the second chorus. Change key up one tone for the final verse (this builds the

---

[26] Praise & Worship series, No. 723.

song further, lifting the spirits of the people) adding a third and even fourth vocal harmony together with touches of trumpet, throwing in the old organ (!) for the third chorus, and then repeat the chorus a final time at a *slower* tempo (this will make its impact greater and grander). At the end of the singing, play out the song with a half-chorus on piano, violin, acoustic guitar and bass and a shimmy on the cymbals.

I'm sure you would have any number of other suggestions, but hopefully you get the idea. **Use the power of the song, and express that power sensibly through the various instruments you have available.** You might not do such a detailed arrangement for every song, but there might be one or two on any given Sunday that you feel could—and should—**provide a high point for the worship**.

I feel I should offer a caution regarding **instrumentals**. A lot of recent songs have their origins in huge congregations with scores of musicians, and many songs are written with those resources in mind—including sometimes lengthy instrumentals. These might work where big bands can carry them, but I sincerely doubt their value as part of most services of worship, even in those big congregations.

Please understand that, as a muso, I love instrumentals when I hear them on a CD. But our purpose is trying to help people worship, and if worship is about *all* the people worshipping God as we have said, then my question about instrumentals is, "What do the people of the congregation do while the musicians are doing their thing?" From my observation, while a few of them get "lost" in the music, many tend to disengage from worship. In most churches I've attended a large number of people stand there looking at each other during instrumentals, wondering when to come back in— especially the many people who are not musically gifted themselves. The key point: **if you break the flow of the people's singing you risk also breaking their focus on**

their worship of God.

Remember, small churches often don't have musicians of sufficient quality to make the musical interludes "work" anyway. Even with great musicians, you need to be sure that the impact *for the worshippers* will be positive. So my advice would be to drop or limit your use of instrumental breaks and keep the people singing.

LINKING SONGS

As we noted earlier, one of the ways of achieving a flowing service is to build musical links between songs that help the congregation stay focussed and make the musical and spiritual transition to the next phase of the worship.

Linking songs is often not hard. **Musical "bridges"**, by which I mean a succession of chords or invented melody that change the mood, tempo, time and key ready for the next song, can link songs together so they flow better. These bridges can be as simple as a single chord, to more elaborate adaptations depending on the changes required. With praise music it can be as simple as a few kicks on the bass drum to set the tempo and everyone is off and clapping. If the rhythm and key are similar—say up a tone—then sometimes a single chord works.

I won't try to explain methods for all situations, but a few simple ones may get you started. The same key, or a tone higher (for example, C to D) is usually easy, as are the fourth and fifth chords of that key. To change up a tone, it's usually possible and easiest to play the fifth chord of the new key and then move into the new key (so, from the key of C to the key of D, play an A chord as the link). Often playing the link chord as a 7th sounds nice (so an A7 in that example). To change to the fourth is also simple. In the key of C, the fourth is F. To change from the key of C to the key of F, you can often simply play a C7 chord (C is the fifth for the key of F) and then begin the new song in F. From C to G, the simple way is to play a D7 chord (which "lifts" a tone from C and is also the fifth chord for the key of G).

Note that it's almost always better to move up a tone than down. This "lifts" the music and encourages the singers. If you are playing a following song in a lower key, it's best to change the key "up" to get there. For example, to get from D to C, rather than simply going from D to C and enduring the "depressed" sound, you might play a progression such as D to G (the fourth for the key of D which is also the fifth for the key of C), then G7 and then C.

Longer links can be developed if it's necessary, that offer more time and space to change elements like the tempo or the time signature (4/4, ¾ etc.).

Even with all those possibilities, there are times when the required songs just won't "merge" simply or in the way you'd hoped. If they won't flow easily, then **create a space** between them—often this can be done with a prayer, a verse of Scripture or a careful phrase from the worship leader.

PRESENTING A SOLO ITEM

Performing a solo in a church service is a wonderful privilege, so treat it as such. **Prepare thoroughly**. Hopefully it's a song you know well and feel confident with. If not, do your homework until you feel competent at least. Learn the song if at all possible. Using sheet music and books has the disadvantage of making you sing down towards it instead of out to the congregation, and is generally less convincing, which may spoil the impact of the message in the song.

Work with the musicians to **produce an arrangement that you are comfortable with**. Make sure the song is within your vocal range, and if it isn't then do something about it. If you can't have it played in a better key, then consider lowering the top note (or raising the bottom one) so that you don't miss the notes and detract from your performance. Check that you are happy with the tempo and volume of your backing music, and rehearse until you are all sure about what you are doing.

As before, remember to **sing to the back** of the congregation. People want to hear your contribution, and looking to the back has the effect of helping everyone feel included—they are either being looked at, or they are closer to the action than those who are.

It's usually better to **stand**. This helps you breathe better and people can see that you are to lead or present something. Sometimes, of course, it can be very effective to have the leader or singer sitting, or even out of sight. Remember that your ultimate purpose is to enhance worship, not get recognised as "the performer". So do what the song, the setting and the intent require.

Practise the look of your performance. Too much movement becomes comical, and not enough makes the performance "wooden". Sing in front of a mirror a few times so you can see what other people will see—and then work to make how you appear and how you gesture authentic for both you and the song.

7 WORSHIP LEADING

Leading people in their worship of God has to be **one of the most awesome privileges on this earth**. Finding ways of helping people to join together to honour their Lord, encouraging them to break down their internal barriers and fully participate, blending the whole with what you do from the front and sending it all heavenward just excites me and humbles me all at once.

There is always something unique and special about a worship time, whether it's a thousand people lifting the roof or a few friends around a campfire. Every time we come into God's presence it's a fresh opportunity to relate to him and do his bidding. There are **always surprises**, no matter how much you have prepared. And that's a good thing: no, it's a wonderful thing, because **in those moments God is flexing his sovereign muscles and tweaking what you're doing** to get it just the way he wants it.

I remember one occasion well, for reasons which will become obvious. It was early in my ordained ministry and I had been asked to lead the worship for a regional gathering of the church. The meeting was packed with people, and being new to the district I probably only knew about four of them! But I had prepared thoughtfully and prayerfully. What would God do with one man and his guitar in this room full of devoted followers of Jesus?

We launched into worship and a few songs later we were blowing the roof off—so much so that the evening's formal business program went out the window. As the singing died down, we were all forming impromptu prayer triplets, encouraging one another in prayer and asking God for healing.

After a long time the leaders came to me and said, "Don, we need to wrap this up: people have to get home tonight." I knew what they meant—I had a 200km drive myself.

As I was pondering how to bring the room back into a final time of focussed worship and "sending out", something really got my attention. I was passed a mobile phone (they were much rarer at that time!) and heard my wife telling me that my dad had died. Now I really needed to end the session, and yet I did not want my own grief to spoil what was still a mind-blowing experience of God in the room.

I said a short silent prayer, and, totally unplanned, found myself strumming a single strong downstroke E chord on my 12-string guitar that resonated around the room and commanded attention. From there, the words "Yes, Jesus loves me!" came out long and slow and strong. We sang the chorus of that beloved hymn very slowly and with increasing power. Then I broke into a faster blues rhythm, adding (occasionally falteringly in my grief) the walking bass on the lower strings of the 12, and the room erupted, "Jesus loves me, this I know..." We sang and sang, repeat after repeat, with people laughing, crying, waving their arms, dancing and hugging one another, all joyously celebrating their walk into the throne-room of heaven—and their emerging from it—deeply in love with their Lord.

Over fifteen years later people will still come up and recall that evening, but I just thank God for the privilege and the amazing way that he prompted me to find the right songs to open up that meeting to him, and, in the midst of my own grief, the perfect means of ending to make the time truly complete. That is **the privilege of a worship leader: to prepare well, to know your job, to deliver it well, and to be on hand as God's vessel to use** in amazing—and unexpected—ways.

Recently I caught the last part of a TV program which had a famous European orchestra playing in an ornate hall in Vienna, with a very famous conductor. The audience were thrilled at what they heard. Then, during the encore piece, the conductor left his post and went around every member of the orchestra, interrupting their playing to greet them and shake their hands. Two things struck me about this. One was that the orchestra played on quite successfully without the conductor—he had prepared them well in rehearsal. But the other thing showed his true worth. Every member of the orchestra greeted the conductor with great honour and reverence, all clearly moved by what they had done together as they thanked him profusely.

As a worship leader, you can be like that conductor. What you do may not be all that apparent. It's not that worship can't go on without you—it can. But many of your fellow performers, both band and congregation, will be deeply grateful for your role when you do it well. And our "audience of one"—the Lord—will show his delight too, in many lovely and unimaginable ways.

What you do as a worship leader affects people. At your best, you can change people's whole perspective on God and their worship of him. You can open doors for them to enter into places they didn't know existed. You can lead and encourage outpourings of faith that will resonate in lives for years—generations even. So—work at your craft. Resolve to be as good at it as you possibly can. Commit it to prayer, and commit it to action.

SKILLS AND TECHNIQUES

Let's look now at what I think are the key attributes of a worship leader. Some of these overlap slightly with your role as a singer or musician, but most are quite distinct because of the special nature of what you do in leading people.

First, remember that **the function of a worship leader is to lead the congregation into the presence of God** so that they can worship him and receive from him. This means working at the conundrum of performing and yet somehow only being visible in those fleeting but crucial linking moments that you are needed. Matt Redman, in his book on worship, said,

> *I often define good worship leaders as those who lead strongly enough so that people follow, but not so strongly that they themselves become the focus.*[27]

Make sure you are well prepared both technically and administratively. Be early and be ready. If you are responsible for the Order of Service, make sure that everyone who needs one has a copy. If you are using data projection or overheads, check that they are organised beforehand and make sure that the person operating them knows what to do. Brief the pastor, the band, the technical team and anyone else who needs to know what you will be doing, and when, and why, and how. **Don't leave things to chance.** I'm not sure if it's the devil or Mr. Murphy and his Law, or maybe both working together, but things left to chance often turn out badly.

Aim to make people relaxed and comfortable in a warm, joyous atmosphere. Work on your stage craft, on the things

---

[27] Matt Redman, *The Unquenchable Worshipper* (2001), Kingsway, Eastbourne, UK, p33.

that you say that welcome and include people; that create a warm and friendly air in the room.

Aim for a sense of expectation. Encourage people to open themselves to all that will happen. Be very positive about the service and about the opportunity that it brings to honour God in a new and unique way.

Aim to give a lead, but not to dominate. We have likened a worship leader to a conductor. Another helpful analogy might be the prompt in a stage show. God is the audience, the congregation are the people on stage, and the worship leader is the prompt helping those on stage to perform better. Though in this case you are necessarily visible, you are seeking to be so unobtrusive that people receive your input without really thinking about who or where it has come from.

Have a set of signals worked out with your band members and those who control the projection so they know what is coming next. Of course, you will have a plan before the service, but there are many times when you want to vary the songs, to repeat a chorus or drop a song out of the list or insert one, even. So help your team know what's coming. I've seen lots of leaders make the shape of a letter "C" with their hand to indicate a chorus, and to arch the back of their hand into a bridge shape to indicate the bridge section of the song. A verse can be indicated with the "V" for victory sign. (One witty leader I saw used the Star Trek salute—using all four fingers with the "V" between the middle and ring fingers!) There are many others.

I won't make any other suggestions as to what you might use. As a guitarist I could never consistently use hand signals like vocalist worship leaders do, so more often than not my team were dependent upon reading one of my weird glances to know that something different was coming! I won't try to describe those expressions, but I give great credit to those playing with me because they nearly always knew what I meant!

Encourage without pressure. Extend an invitation to people to take hold of their worship and expand their horizons in their praise. And don't ever, ever chastise. Telling people off for poor effort just destroys any sense of worship.

I learned that lesson way back in my home church when I was about 15 years old. Our regular minister was away, and the man replacing him that day had chosen an opening hymn that nobody knew. We had a choir, but they didn't seem to know it either. We were struggling through the second verse when the man interrupted. I thought to myself that he was going to change to a hymn we knew, but instead he chastised the whole congregation for lack of effort and enthusiasm and made us start again—the old, "once more with feeling" command. I don't remember the man's name, I don't remember his sermon, I don't even remember which hymn it was—but I shall never forget the telling off we got, and the terrible feeling we all had because of it. It still makes me cringe over 40 years later. However poor it may have been, **worship is never, repeat never, enhanced through the use of guilt and shame.**

Instead, **encourage people into worship**: tell them to lift their voices, to praise their God, to honour Jesus and to join their hearts together. Phrases like these encourage people into the worship.

Encouragement is helpful especially **when a song is new**. Actually, I rarely said: "This is a new song", because it stops half the people from trying to sing it! If the band knows it and you lead it well they will soon catch on, and assume that it's only them who doesn't know it.

Give clear instructions where they are necessary, but **be careful of talking too much—when in doubt, say less rather than more**. Leading worship is not about you, or what happened to you last week or on the way into church. It's about the precious foot-soldiers of Jesus in front of you, and helping them to worship their Lord. So don't talk more than you need to.

And **don't be afraid of silence**. If you've led worship for even a few weeks you will probably already have experienced a point at which God is ministering to his people, and the best thing you can do as a leader is let him! Give people time to sense the Lord's presence and feel his touch on them. And when the time seems right, find a gentle, helpful way of moving on.

Be very careful with jokes—even the most innocuous and happy story can find people who will misinterpret it. I remember a pastor making a joke about how he taught the worship leader everything she knew, and even though he immediately said he was joking, people were muttering about him being big-headed! Over time you will discern where the boundaries are with humour. Always adhere to them. Stay well within those borders so that your understated good humour adds to the corporate desire to be there, without setting people murmuring about the "clown" at the front.

Avoid jargon. The church is full of special language, and it's easy to extol the jubilation of sanctification, justification, being redeemed by the blood of the Lamb and being found in him, but you will not just confuse visitors, you'll have half the regular members wondering what you meant. And be careful not just of "Christianese", but any jargon from the worlds of music, IT, football or anywhere else. Keep your language simple and clear.

At all times **make sure you are watching and listening to what is happening**. You need to be fully aware of where the music is going and what's happening with the people. Look for deliberate signals from the other participants and the minister/pastor/priest, and watch for movements of heads, eyes, and arms.

Sometimes **crises occur while you are leading**. Be aware so that you can make a proper call about how to continue. Sometimes people fall down, and it could be under the power of the Spirit, through a faint, or a collapse from a heart attack. From the front you can't tell. Usually there is an immediate response from people nearby. I assume that they can make a better call than I can from the front, so I make it a rule to **carry on unless there is an obvious need to interrupt the worship**. If someone waves at you with wild gestures telling you to stop, then that's probably a good idea, but otherwise I assume that people nearby can get all the help they need without intervention from the front.

Sometimes it helps if you happen to know the person. I had a lady in one of my churches who blacked out perhaps three or four times a year. It was caused by a medical condition with an unpredictable onset. If I saw her go down, I knew I could safely carry on because her husband and friends knew what to do.

Of course, something very serious may cause **enough of a commotion to interrupt** a significant number of people. In cases like that my usual advice would be to **offer prayer for the person and those assisting, and then to move on** as soon as practical to do so.

Remember that **the minister/pastor/priest ultimately controls the service** (unless you have some internal agreement to the contrary). So be their servant. Let them have the final say on how long the worship is and when it's time to move on. Think of yourself as their instrument.

Make sure that you are constantly attuned to the mood of the worship. What you had hoped for may not be forthcoming, or maybe it's all going amazingly and you want to throw in an extra chorus, or break for prayer, or add a Bible verse and a song repeat. **You are the one who creates and sustains the flow and direction** at this point. You take hold of all the careful planning and the rehearsal and the skill of the band, and you shape the worship. **You link the songs; you offer images from Scripture; you focus the intentions of the gathered people**. You are the one who is making the connections, plucking the verses from God's tree of wisdom, mixing together the words just sung with the ones to come and blending them into a sweet journey into the throne-room of God.

You can't do those things well without your own deep relationship with the Lord and a serious time of preparation both logistically and prayerfully. And you need to **stay deeply connected to what God is doing** in the room. You have the call to lengthen the present moment and revel in it, or to move on to the next phase of the journey in a way that builds both the expectation and the richness of the movement as each new song enlarges the experience and focuses God's people more deeply on him.

This one almost goes without saying—but it's crucial, so I'll spell it out. *Be sure you are worshipping*—**you can't lead others into something you are not doing yourself**. We have used the images of the conductor of the orchestra and the prompt in the theatre. Now think of yourself as the butler who opens the door to the throne-room of God's palace. The butler works there; he knows his way around. He knows which door is which, and he knows which doors he should open and when he should open them. So when God says, "Open the door and bring my people in to Me", you are the one who gets the privilege of standing and saluting the saints as they enter into God's presence. But you can't do that if you're running up from behind trying to get through the crowd. And, as the responsible doorman that day, the door may not open unless you are there to do it. You are the one controlling and co-ordinating the practical, the musical, and to some extent the spiritual elements that might allow that door to open.

Matt Redman quotes an anonymous friend who said to him, "Be the lead worshipper as well as the worship leader."[28] He thought at the time that it was just a clever play on words, but afterwards he got the point. I believe that if you are not worshipping then there is a grave risk that what takes place through you will be little more than a carefully choreographed concert. I'm not saying that God can't work in spite of you, but the reality is that if you are the chosen instrument that day and you are not worshipping, then it's highly likely that many others will copy you and will not worship too—and the whole service could fall flat. If you are worshipping then doors are opened and God's Spirit is fully released to inspire the worship of the people.

PRESENCE

I know we're seeking God's presence, but we need to think about yours too. **Your presence—your level of involvement, confidence and interaction as a worship leader—needs to be at the right level.** Over-confidence and under-confidence are equally problematic. If you are over-confident you risk taking over and turning it all into a show. If you lack confidence the congregation don't get the lead they need to walk the journey with you, and the worship will lack a strong focus and tend to wander in its intent. So let's aim now to pitch your own presence at the right level.

First, **be enthusiastic and friendly**. Your confidence in what is to come needs to show through so that people will want to

---

[28] Anonymous, quoted in Redman, *The Unquenchable Worshipper*, Kingsway 2001, p41-42.

"join up" for the journey. Let your joy in the Lord show. That's not to be artificial either. If the congregation is in mourning because someone's baby died, don't hit them in the face with happy-clappy stuff—it will appear shallow and uncaring. But routinely aim for an inviting and joyful atmosphere in the way you start out.

The immediate counterbalance to that is, of course, that you **don't try to be a star**. You are inviting people to join you in worshipping God, not asking them to look at you trying to be cool. At all times you need to stay sensitive.

As a general rule my advice is **not to apologise for mistakes**. Most of the time the apology becomes more of a distraction to the worship than the mistake was. People know that we all make them, so correct only what really needs correction in the simplest way possible and move on.

For some people the responsibility seems great and they feel inadequate. Don't. **Your people, and your pastor, have placed trust in you, so they recognise your gifts. And the Lord surely does**—he gave them to you! What you are doing might seem really challenging, but take heart and learn, from God and from the others. If your heart is focussed on him he will find the way for you.

Perhaps you are someone who has not yet realised the significance of the role you carry. **Don't ever think of yourself as just the next person on the roster** or that you're just filling in while someone else is away. Remember, this is a ministry that is from God and is significant for every person who comes that day, so take on the role responsibly and prayerfully.

So it's OK to be confident in your own ability—confidence releases that ability—but remember always that this is God's house and God's people. So believe deeply in his presence with you and seek **the Holy Spirit's help**. Your abilities, be they great or small, will only ever get you part of the way. That's why **a healthy dose of humility is crucial** to the role, because then you will leave room for the Holy Spirit to move and inspire both you and the people. The Holy Spirit will want to use you, and both big-headedness and timidity will hinder him. An oversized ego won't leave him anywhere to move, while being too timid to follow his promptings will limit things as well. So—**believe in your God-given abilities, yet be humble and ready to follow the Spirit's lead.**

If ever you are wondering how it all might be coming across, you don't need to wait until afterwards for feedback from others. **When in doubt, concentrate on worship**—first yourself, and then gently bringing people with you. If you were worried about grandstanding, that will cure it. If your worry was about lack of confidence, then immersing yourself in worship will also cure it. Set yourself on being the lead worshipper, and trust God to help you with the rest. He will!

THE WORSHIP LEADER'S TEN COMMANDMENTS

Having said all of that, worship leaders don't have to be perfect. They don't even have to be singers! I have known some very gifted leaders who were not musical, but could direct a service well and had a good sense of flow and direction. In some churches you may have limited resources, but someone who is not competent as a singer can still do an excellent job of leading worship when they have a heart for Jesus and a feel for how worship happens.

So, in light of that I thought I'd have a go at listing what I really think are the key attributes of a worship leader. See how you react to these:

1. Be committed to Christ.
2. Be humble and sensitive to the leading of the Holy Spirit.
3. Believe that God's presence and power is manifest in

worship music and prayer.
4. Develop skill in holding rhythm and tune.
5. Develop a clear speaking and singing voice.
6. Be a servant of the preacher/pastor.
7. Be an encourager.
8. Be dedicated to your role.
9. Be prepared to be vulnerable.
10. Be the lead worshipper.

8 OTHER WORSHIP MINISTRIES

There are a number of platform roles that are performed by a range of people, and other roles of a technical nature performed from the back or elsewhere, and all of **these roles impact the flow, direction and power of the service**.

I'm only going to address the roles that directly impact the actual worship time. I assume your church can plan and implement strategies for welcoming and caring for newcomers (and their cars), children, older folk and many others who enter your premises. They are beyond the scope of this book. I want to help with the actual service and those who make it work well.

I should add that in some ways it's quite presumptuous of me to comment on some of the following areas, because I only have a very small personal experience in some of them. But it's important for you that I do. That's because I'm talking about your area of ministry from the point of view of a pastor or minister, and as you are the person responsible for a particular and important part of worship, **you need to know what your pastor is looking for from your role**, and how your performance of it might impact other people, or the overall flow and impact of the service.

So read the information below in that light. I won't cover the technical detail of the technical roles, but I can tell you from my experience what helps and what doesn't from the broader perspective of what your minister/priest/pastor might be hoping for.

BIBLE READER

For most of the twenty centuries of the church, the average churchgoer was illiterate and the only way they got to hear the word of God was when someone read it. Today in the Western world we have Bibles by the dozen in our homes to read whenever we want. But the sad fact is that most of them lie unread on a bookshelf. So it remains that when you read the Bible in church on Sunday you are helping people to take in the Word and achieve for them what they seem unable to do for themselves.

But it's more than that. When we hear the Bible read in church it's like we are all being nourished together by God's Word. It is a communal affirmation of what we believe, a joint reassurance of the precepts by which we choose to live our lives.

So reading from the Scriptures for your congregation is **a privilege and honour.** Treat it that way by giving it your best.

Practise your reading several times until you are thoroughly familiar with it. Take note of any complex words—some biblical names are tricky—and get them right. Work at it until you feel confident of the sense of the passage.

This especially applies if your church wants you to read from an older translation, like King James. It's a bit like reading Shakespeare—you have to let the words sink in a bit before you are sure what it is saying. Once you've practised and you know what is being said it helps you to get the inflections right in the way you read it, so that people hearing it will have the best chance of following you.

Having said that, **my strong advice is to read from an**

accurate modern translation. If you are free to select your own translation, then choose one that is accurate and clear. In my understanding the most accurate are the New International Version (NIV), the English Standard Version (ESV), and the New Revised Standard Version (NRSV). For a very readable Bible (though not quite as precise in translation) you could try the New Living Translation (NLT) or the Contemporary English Version (CEV) while The Message is a popular modern paraphrase (not a tight translation at all, but one that tries to convey the same meaning in a modern way).

Stand near the **microphone** and speak into it. Adjust its height and angle if necessary. Many news reporters on TV hold the microphone well away from their mouths, but they are using a different (and very expensive) type of microphone unsuited to singing and other church purposes. So don't copy them! Get up close—within 2–3cm—to the mic and aim it at your mouth. **Being too far away is the usual cause of feedback** and other problems. It's much harder for the sound technician to adjust your volume if the microphone is too far from you.

Speak slowly! Nerves often make us talk faster. Take your time and be clear. Remember to breathe! Use appropriate emphasis. If there is speech from one of the people named within the reading, then speak it as it might have been spoken. If the events are dramatic, then use tone, volume and pitch that bring it out. That's not to say you should turn it into a drama—leave that to plays and actors—but bring out the drama or the speech in a way that makes the reading alive and helps it to convey its message.

If the reading is poetry, then read it that way. Hebrew poetry, like the Psalms and much of the writings of the prophets, often contains couplets, where the second line repeats in slightly different language the meaning of the first line. In

Proverbs we find a counterbalancing phrase, such as, "A righteous person does this, but a wicked person will do that." When you see these sorts of things happening it will probably change the way you say it.

Announce where the reading is from and the translation you are using. Many churches use a particular translation and place copies of it in the seats. If that is the case, make sure you read the passage from that Bible and be ready to tell people the page number when you introduce it. Not everyone can find Micah or Titus quickly when they want to! Visitors might not know if a book is in the Old or New Testament, so help them out. Repeat the reference in case people missed the detail. This information also now often appears via the data projector.

Occasionally some context for the reading is helpful, but check with the preacher before you go into any long explanations of it. You are not there to give the sermon! Some readers go to great length to explain where the reading comes from, what was happening just before it, and what it all led to. But ultimately that's the preacher's job. He or she may want to use the passage in ways you haven't considered. Some people's introductions can take longer than the reading, and they can unwittingly discourage other readers who feel less competent to offer such lengthy explanations. So the simple solution is to just do what you're asked to do—read the passage.

End appropriately. It's usually quite simple to indicate that the end of a reading is approaching by your tone, emphasis and slower speed of delivery. People quickly realise you are concluding. In some churches there are liturgical responses for the congregation after readings. If so, then use them.

PRAYER LEADER

Leading your fellow Christians in prayer to God is an awesome thing. To interpret the concerns of the world and present the longings of God's people to him; to express their joint love and devotion to the Lord; to pour out on their behalf their distress and admit their failings and disobedience; and to plead their case for the outpouring of grace, compassion and mercy—surely these are responsibilities and privileges of a high order and carry immense and deep spiritual importance.

It follows then, that whatever your own background, whatever style of worship you come from, if you are praying on behalf of God's people, it is vital that **your prayers are ones to which the people can say, "Amen"**. This marvellous ancient Hebrew word, "Amen" which spilled over into Aramaic and Greek doesn't have a true English equivalent, but in the Bible it gets translated as "truly" or "truthfully" ("verily" in the King James Bible), and also means something like, "let it be so" or "Yes, I agree".

Public prayers need to cover subjects that are on the people's hearts, and to do so in ways they can connect with instantly— because you are asking them to hear them and give assent to them instantly. For the congregation to "stay with you" as you pray, you have to be praying about things that are important to them, and doing it in a way they understand and appreciate. I think that public prayer is more powerful when the congregation is "tuned in" and really praying the prayer word by word with the leader. Anything that hinders that connection weakens the prayer.

So if you are praying a prayer on behalf of others, take care how you word it. For example, if you pray a prayer asking that a particular political party win an election, there might be half the people present who do not agree with the prayer. When praying for elections, its best to pray that God would grant the nation wise and godly leadership through whoever wins—everyone can say "Amen" to that. Equally with other potentially divisive subjects, it is sufficient—and often best—to **raise the issue with God and leave it in his hands**, without trying to forecast a particular outcome.

Know the scope of the prayer you have been asked to lead. Is it adoration, or confession, or thanksgiving, or offertory, or intercession, or for some other purpose? If you're given the role of praising and thanking God, it's <u>not</u> the time to pray for Aunt Sally's hernia, or for world peace, the government or even your pastor. Those are petitions and come in the intercessory (asking) prayer.

Think about **the context of your prayer** in the service. Does it come as part of the worship phase, or following the singing but before the preaching, or after the preaching or where? Think about how you might link what has been happening in the service with what you are to pray. Think about how you might end the prayer such that it leads into what follows. If the service has an overall theme, think about how your prayer fits into that.

How long are you being asked to pray for? Some prayers should be short, and other situations seem to require a longer time. For example, a prayer for the offering is usually brief, while adoration and intercession are longer. A prayer of commissioning needs to pray for the person being commissioned, the role they will take, the influences upon that role and the people connected to it—so there is a bit to cover. But it should still be of reasonable length and not excessive. Don't ramble on for the sake of it. **Pray what needs to be prayed and then thank God that he cares for us, and then close**. Intercessory prayers (supplications, petitions, prayers for others) could go on forever. You need to be selective. Sometimes having a theme—especially if it is related to the theme of the day—is helpful.

Prepare thoroughly. Very few people can stand up and pray publicly without giving careful thought to it. That doesn't mean you have to write it out and read it, unless you want to approach it that way. Be careful if you write your prayer out in full because sometimes that can sound artificial and stilted—not because what you have written is dull, but because we generally write in a slightly different way than we speak. But make some notes in general terms at least, so you know what you intend to say.

If you are required to read a written prayer from a book, prepare it thoroughly so you know exactly where to put inflections and pauses. Stumbling over a written prayer can make it seem artificial to the listener.

Speak slowly and clearly, and stay close to the microphone if there is one. You are praying on behalf of others, so allow them to hear and follow what you pray. Mumbled or rushed prayers don't allow the people to participate or empower the prayer.

Use common language. Archaic language is no more holy than present day English—so don't use it. The daily prayer in the Australian Parliament opens with, "Almighty God, we humbly beseech thee that thou mightst vouchsafe this thy parliament…" and it doesn't surprise me that some people want to abolish it. It's hard enough for Christians to work out what is being said, let alone an atheist!

There is also the slight possibility that the person praying in "religious language", whether modern or archaic, is doing so for subconscious reasons of pride. Ask yourself why you use those words. If, deep down, it's because "I can do it and it makes me look good, or sound important, or sound spiritual, or…" then there's almost certainly a pride issue for you to think about. The short, simple answer is to speak so that those you are praying on behalf of can understand what you are saying to God for them.

Don't repeat God's name incessantly. Some people use the word "Lord" or "Jesus" like punctuation in their prayer— DON'T. It's distracting, it's poor English, and you don't normally talk like that. **Talk to God the way you might talk to your best friend**, because that's who he is. And if your best friend's name was Michael, you probably wouldn't say things like, "Hi Michael, it's so great to see you Michael, and Michael, I really want to thank you, Michael, for all you did last week, Michael, because, Michael, it helped me so much, dear Michael." Get the point? I think of it like this. We have an immense privilege in calling God Father, and his Son Jesus as Lord. Privileges shouldn't be abused. So we use the names we have been given for God thankfully and frequently, but we don't wear them out!

Somewhat strangely, an issue has emerged about praying for **God's will** to be done. People will say that God has given us a mind to think with, and he has invited us to pour out our desires to God in prayer. Completely true. The argument then goes that if you simply pray, "Lord if it be your will, then please do this…", it is a "weak" prayer. It isn't being bold enough to say what it is that you need God to do for you. It isn't a prayer that prays in faith, believing the words of Jesus that what we ask for will be done.

I am not so sure about that last part. It's not that we don't want to ask God for what we think we need, it's because of our belief that God's ways are best and we want to align ourselves with him.

Jesus himself clearly put the will of the Father ahead of anything else. He said in John's Gospel, *"My food…is to do the will of him who sent me…"* (John 4:34, my emphasis). In the Garden of Gethsemane he prayed, *"My Father, if it is possible, may this cup be taken from me. Yet not as I will, but as you will."*

130

(Matthew 26:39, my emphasis). And he taught us to pray, *"Your will be done on earth as it is in heaven."* (Matthew 6:10, my emphasis).

I fully accept that God allows us to speak boldly and plainly to him. We can ask for what we want, just as Jesus did in Gethsemane. But Jesus quickly and ultimately sought the will of the Father, and so should we. Are we that naïve—or arrogant—to think that our ways are better than God's? If we want our way and not God's, have we truly "died to self"?

Of course we can tell God what we would like, but never be afraid or embarrassed to pray that God, in his sovereignty and wisdom, might prevail in any and every situation. As disciples of Jesus, we should be honoured to pray as he taught us and **ask that the Father's will be done on earth as it is in heaven**—even if his will seems like it could unfold to our personal cost. **There is nothing weak or immature about that prayer**: quite the contrary, in fact, as Jesus showed us in Gethsemane.

Close your prayer in the name of Jesus. It is he who has done what was needed to give us access to the Father, so when we say, "in Jesus' name we pray," it's not like putting a stamp on a letter, it's like, "the only reason we could ever assume you would bother with this stuff is because Jesus tells us that what we think and want is important to him". Jesus sits at the right hand of God and intercedes for us. When we pray, "through Jesus Christ our Lord" it's because Jesus is the one who has made it possible to ask the Father.

If you are to lead the **Lord's Prayer**, then do so methodically, in its familiar phrase by phrase format. Make sure you are praying the version commonly used in that church, be it traditional or modern. Don't try anything fancy. I have heard people change the phrasing, mess with the speed and tone of the prayer and all that eventuates is confusion and frustration. Again, you are not there to be clever or show off how individual you are. Bless the worshippers by giving them a strong and measured vocal lead so that all may participate and pray to their Lord.

DATA PROJECTIONIST

When I was a kid in church my brother and I used to sit together with our family, and usually there weren't enough hymn books and we had to share. Inevitably there were problems because whichever one of us was holding the book would not hold it still enough for the other to read. Perhaps the key role for the data projectionist is that of "holding the book". **Everyone in the church is dependent upon your ability to put the right words on the screen in time** for them to be sung.

When I think about overhead projectors I still have nightmares about the time I was belatedly thrust into the role for a large and important (and amazingly, a bit disorganised) ordination service. Less than 15 minutes before the start, in an unfamiliar church full of people, I was appointed the projectionist, given a mismatched set of slides and asked to "go find the projector". That seemingly simple task took twelve of the remaining minutes (it turned out to be upstairs in a locked storeroom) and I barely had time to get it shining in the right direction before we started. Because the slides were of varying font sizes and physical dimensions, some with cardboard frames and some without, putting the right words up clearly and in time to be sung was traumatic indeed, as was moving the slides smoothly between verses of the songs. I have rarely worked so hard in church—and the only feedback I got was negative comment about the words sliding off the glass at the wrong time.

As for data projectors, we have probably all experienced the Sunday where the computer wouldn't start, or wouldn't read the song file, or froze on the first screen, or (name your disaster here). Every pair of eyes in the place is watching your every move, and the moment something goes wrong all those eyes turn to the desk.

So my first piece of advice is: don't assume you can do it— it's NOT as easy as it looks! **Know your equipment** and the programs that run on it, **and test it all** thoroughly before you start.

Be early. Arriving at the last minute and depending upon someone else to have gotten things ready is asking for a problem.

Be prepared—make sure you have all the song files (or overheads), and that they're in the right sequence. If you are the person who prepares the slides, **make sure that the words are set out as they are supposed to be sung**, so that people can see the rhythm and rhyme of the words. If the rhyming word is halfway through a line the people gain no sense of how the song should flow musically.

Be there for the music rehearsal so that you can follow through the Order of Service and all the songs and other material to be projected, and ensure that all the words are there, in the right sequence. It helps enormously if you **know the songs**—be aware of the usual pattern of chorus, repeated sections and endings—so that if something is varied by the worship leader—or goes wrong—you have the ability to get the right material on the screen as quickly as possible.

Part of being prepared is to **be ready for last minute changes**. I've seen some amazing feats of dexterity performed by data projectionists! The worship leader suddenly launches into a song not on the play list for that day. It has to be found in the system, brought into the list, and projected—hopefully with an appropriate background—in a matter of seconds. When you can do that sort of thing fluently you are earning your pay!

Photographs or other **backgrounds for lyric slides need to be subtle**—related to the theme of the song but simple enough to allow the words easy visibility and not be distracting. I've seen a number of churches using a moving background—for example, of waves breaking on a beach or clouds sailing past a mountaintop. Personally I find these distracting. I remember during the thirteenth or fourteenth repeat of one song I caught myself finding the point in the picture when it "looped" and started again. For me, the fact that I lost focus on my worship of God makes me rate that as a problem, however overdone the song had become. The fact that a technological trick is possible doesn't necessarily mean its use is wise. Be careful.

It's crucial to **get the words up on time**. A song will die instantly if the next line is not there in time to be sung. Opinions will vary about when the "right" time is. In my view, it should be around a half-second or more before the words have to be used, so people can take in what is coming next. Yet it's important not to cut off the previous line before it is finished. Exactly at the time they are to be sung is too late, I think. People need that instant to mentally prepare to sing the next line. On the other hand, if the words are up too early before the commencement of a song it can be distracting from what the worship leader might be saying or praying, so learn to interpret the signs and know when to click the "go" button.

If you are still using an overhead, keep movements of the words to a minimum, and do them smoothly and precisely, at the end of a line or verse (ready for the next one). Make the move swift and accurate and then leave it alone—small "adjustments" are distracting.

Don't try to put the whole song on the screen at once. Get your pastors and worship leaders to agree on a font size that makes the words accessible to all—some people have glasses and other vision impairment. And remember that people at the back may only be able to see the top couple of lines over the heads of those in front of them. **How much to project in one screen is a trade-off between font size, visibility and the flow of the song**. I like to have enough of a song projected to allow the worshippers to see and know what they are singing. One or two lines at a time often does not allow this, so I try to have the screen showing a reasonable amount without sacrificing the font size.

Finally—and this is probably already obvious—**be a willing servant** of those who need you to do well: the worship-leader, the singers and musicians, the preacher, and especially the people who have come to worship God.

THE SOUND DESK

From a minister's perspective, the two nightmares of the sound system are the howl of feedback, and people looking blankly toward the front or the sound desk and muttering, "We can't hear."

So my first request of my sound engineers was that they **know the system**. If you don't know the volume knob from the reverb, seek some training so that you are competent and confident.

My other major concern over sound I have mentioned already, and that is that those at the sound desk have a huge responsibility to the worshipping community to get the level right. **The volume used for worship is crucial**. Worship is NOT a rock concert, however much the band at the front might want to immerse the room in their sound.

It's important that singers and instruments can be heard so they can lead the people. But the people also need to be able to hear themselves. **If they can't hear themselves, and have no sense that they are adding to the music by participating, the congregation STOP SINGING**. When this happens the whole point of them being in a service of worship is undermined. By all means seek a rich and full sound from the voices and instruments you have available, but **do not ever dominate the congregation** with the overall volume. The people MUST be able to add their part to the whole if corporate worship is to be worship and not a concert.

From my perspective, the best advice I can give you is to **be prepared**. That means leaving as little as possible to chance— check cables, connections, batteries, and everything else that might be a source of trouble. **Test everything**.

Part of being prepared will mean **attending any music and drama rehearsals** so you know what's coming and so that potential problems can be sorted out beforehand. Of course, it will also help them get their contributions right if the equipment is working as it will be during the service.

Do a sound check. Different singers and speakers will need different levels, and they may well be passing a mic from one to another. Perhaps the same person may need a different level from last time. Some sound engineers keep notes on various people and settings, and I have seen instructions taped near the slider on the mixer for a frequent speaker.

Often folk on the sound desk these days are involved in recording the service for distribution as a CD, DVD or MP3 file or other online formats. Remember that the church has significant obligations under the copyright laws for how these things are done. Make yourself aware of the rules and ensure that proper records are kept of what has been recorded and what modes and numbers of distribution have occurred.

Finally—as always—**be a willing servant**. A service of

worship is not the time to experiment with weird effects! The sound system is there to help people hear and worship and to increase the effectiveness of those who lead, so apply your technical skill to achieving that to the best of your ability and the system's capacity, and you will have served well.

A FEW THOUGHTS FOR THE PASTOR

My ordained and/or employed brothers and sisters, I won't try to tell you how to do your job. I hope that what I have offered here will enhance your own skills and thoughts on service design and delivery. Whether we are ordained or not, the principles are the same, from the more complex notions of direction and flow to the simple skill of holding a microphone. Let me add just a couple of lessons that I learned, sometimes painfully, in my time of professional ministry. You are welcome to apply them or ignore them—your choice—but given that your people will probably read this bit too, it might be wise to have your thoughts together on the stuff I raise!

In one church I was in I made the mistake of **not really training anyone in platform ministry**. I enjoyed myself leading things my way. When I went away on holidays there were stories that my lay replacements had struggled a bit. But instead of teaching them I ignored the problem. When I left that congregation there were serious challenges for the church over their ability to conduct worship in the way I had made them accustomed to. I had set them a great example—except that all they ever did was to watch. They never had the chance to really try and do it while under my guidance. My fault.

I also hadn't taught anyone there enough about **service planning**—maybe writing this book is partly to salve my conscience! I could do the planning easily, so I did. And, looking back, I have to admit that, **in my pride, I thought I**

could do it best—so I didn't let anyone else try.

Finally, in my busy parish life, often I found myself **operating as a last-minute person**—which, if I did things myself, I could get away with. Involving other people takes time and effort, and better planning. I should have done more of it. Instead I took the quick, easy and lazy option.

I remember another occasion early in my ministry handing over the leadership of the service to my team-in-training, and they did a good job. Then I stood up to preach the sermon and—as it was explained to me afterwards—**undermined everything they had done** in leading worship to that point. First, I welcomed everyone. Then I thanked the team. Then I prayed. Finally I did what I had stood up to do: I preached.

When we talked about it afterwards, they gently explained to me how the congregation and visitors had already been welcomed. I didn't need to do it again. **It made it seem like their welcome didn't matter** and that only my welcome as the professional was good enough. I shuddered.

My thanks to them—well intentioned—**made them feel like a bunch of amateurs** who were being patted on the head like children. It made it seem like only when I stood up would the "proper service" begin. I cringed.

Surely they couldn't criticise my prayer? But they had already prayed for the preaching of the Word, so **it was like their prayers were somehow unworthy** and only mine would be acceptable to God. I groaned.

My role in that service was to preach, not to provide a **running commentary on what had gone before**. I had behaved like a teacher in school offering qualified praise for the test results and then telling everyone what the right answers were. I negated all that had been offered to that point. Good or bad (and it had been good) I should have accepted what had been done as our team's offering to God and his people that day, and simply done the team thing—preach my message.

When you involve lay people in the church's ministry you trust them to play their part. And if you want to welcome everyone or pray, then take those roles in the service plan— don't double up on what has been done well by others already. **And the time for coaching is before and after, not during the service**. As you can see, I was the one who learned the biggest lessons afterwards!

OK, I hope from the rest of the book that you'll work out that I wasn't a total failure. I did do a lot of things that turned out OK. But my point is that when you encourage your people to take part—as I believe you should—then it takes effort and sacrifice on your part. You have to take the time and trouble to teach your team about worship, and service construction, and platform ministry. And you have to **be a team player yourself**, and not put yourself in any way above them through careless words and actions.

Accept their gifts, delight in them, and add your own. The end result will be far greater than you thought possible. And the Lord will be smiling.

A FINAL WORD...

Most people learn to worship by being in the midst of other worshippers. If the worship around them is passionate then the chances are that new people will learn to worship deeply and expressively. If, when they look around, those near them are clearly only "going through the motions" or, worse, appearing uninterested or bored or disconnected, then new people learn that behaviour too. My prayer is that, as you take hold of some new insights from what you have read, you will ensure you are a passionate worshipper and inspire your church to passionate worship as well.

Your congregation will feel more inclined toward worship when the service is well-planned, flowing and directed toward its theme. Almost without knowing why, they will start to move with the flow of the service, take in more of what is said, feel more refreshed afterwards and retain more for longer in the coming week when their experience of worship is positive and helpful.

And **your people will warm to worship when they are invited, included and encouraged**. Your task as a worship planner and leader is to involve the whole congregation in what is happening, not to mount some kind of spectacle of tradition or upbeat multi-media extravaganza. Worship is the privilege of all God's children, and one of the primary roles of those conducting it is to make it inclusive and participatory.

I hope, as you have read through this little guide, that you have picked up on my passion for worship. I love to worship

God, and I really love being in the midst of a room full of Jesus' disciples who are giving their all in their love for Jesus. Especially I have loved the times when I could lead with my voice and trusty old Maton 12-string guitar and encourage congregations to draw closer to Jesus in song.

I've mentioned earlier that I had to retire from full time parish ministry. As I write this, it is over three years since I was diagnosed with Motor Neurone Disease (MND) and about four years since the first symptoms. A terminal illness with no known cure, no remissions and little treatment, MND destroys the nerves that control the body's motor skills— everything from walking and writing to talking, swallowing and even breathing. It moves unpredictably in the body, gradually reducing your capacity to live. In some patients it acts quite rapidly, and other (rarer) times more slowly. The average life-expectancy is twenty-seven months. I'm a slow one, or as I prefer to think of it, a walking miracle!

In my case, the first symptom was slurred speech. As my tongue withered I lost the ability to sing and then talk—hence my retirement. Eating has become more and more difficult, and I now have a feeding tube direct into my stomach. I am beginning to lose strength in my legs and arms. My left hand is struggling to play chords fast enough and firmly enough on the guitar neck. I still play in the church band as they lovingly tolerate my fumbles, but without the Lord's intervention my days there are tightly numbered too.

I'm not telling you all this to extract sympathy. I am at peace with God. Jesus is the Lord of my life and he can heal it or take it according to his needs and purposes.

But what I am saying is that unless the Lord intervenes, my turn is over. I can't get up and demonstrate these skills anymore. I have set out to put into print the things I have learned as clearly as I can. I hope they inspire you and help you. Now it is up to you, and others rising around you, to learn the skills and take your corner of the worshipping church on from here. **Take your role seriously, fulfil it willingly, minister lovingly and worship humbly.**

As for me,

> *I am already being poured out like a drink offering... I have fought the good fight. I have finished the race. I have kept the faith. Now there is in store for me the crown of righteousness... (2 Timothy 4:6-8)*

Over to you: may God bless you richly as you minister in his Church and among your fellow children of the Lord!

Don Purdey

Adelaide

July 2014

POSTSCRIPT

This book is an expression of Don's love of God, and Don's passion for worship and ministry. It is an honest and inspiring account of the joys and challenges faced by worship leaders. It's also an encouragement and reminder to each of us to set our eyes clearly on Jesus—to undergird our lives and leadership styles with a personal relationship with our Saviour Jesus. May you be encouraged by my husband's words, and his heart for worshipping God.

WITH THANKS...

On behalf of Don and myself, I want to thank all the wonderful people who have helped us get this book to print. To the many family and friends who have provided support and encouragement throughout this process, and for those who have read through and given feedback on this book.

To our children (Jill, Belle, Ian, Malcolm and Ruth) and their spouses for the invaluable support, patience, proofreading help and encouragement. Special thanks to Malcolm and Ruth, I am indebted to you both! To Ruth for the amazing cover design and amended title (Don would have loved it!); for the website, marketing help and ongoing support. To Malcolm for the skilled assistance with grammar, writing, hours of humour-filled formatting and a great Preface!

To Craig Bailey for writing the Foreword, such a beautiful tribute to Don and his book. To Jess Foster and Greg

Anderson for the meticulous proofreading efforts and enthusiasm! To Sandy Craig for all the encouragement, advice and wisdom. To Dora Stewart and the other staff at Openbook Howden Print and Design for the professional advice and generous service in printing this book.

Blessings,

Annette Purdey

September 2020

ABOUT THE AUTHOR

Don Purdey had a life-long passion for music and worship. A self-taught guitarist, he won awards as a child performer and later on the ABC TV talent show, *Quest*. An after-hours career as a singer became the training ground and springboard for his passion for worship leading, and he led bands in many churches over three decades. He also wrote many worship songs, including one chosen for a national youth conference.

Before entering the ministry he worked as secretary of Australia's counter-terrorism coordination committee in Canberra. Following God's call into ordained ministry, he moved to Adelaide in 1994 with his wife and young family to study a Bachelor of Ministry.

His ministry was marked by encouraging others and sharing his faith in God through his leadership, preaching, and worship leading. He also wrote a series of articles, published in a national church magazine, *ACC Catalyst*. In retirement Don turned his writing skills in a new direction, earning a Graduate Certificate in Creative Writing. While he also had a fictional work published, *Don't Fret* resulted from material he formulated during his ministry over many years.

Don retired early due to Motor Neurone Disease, which caused progressive loss of his speech and singing voice. Yet, a new and powerful phase of his ministry emerged as people now listened more carefully. It was not only because they had to (as Don was losing his speech) but because they appreciated his faith-giving insights, humour and wisdom borne from trusting God through hardship. In the latter months Don communicated through a speech program (on his iPad) or by writing, and he continued to live courageously, adapting to reduced physical abilities and drawing even closer to God.

On 23rd July 2014 Don went to be with the Lord, he died suddenly whilst picking a rose. He had been making the finishing touches to this book on that day. Don is survived by his wife Annette, 5 adult children and their spouses, with 17 grandchildren and counting!

Enjoy this book?

ORDER ONE FOR A FRIEND AT
dontfretbook.com

Practical advice on worship—from service planning to when your sheet music falls in a heap

SCAN TO ORDER